ELECTION

Diary
of an
ELECTION

WITH MARGARET THATCHER ON THE CAMPAIGN TRAIL

A PERSONAL ACCOUNT BY

CAROL THATCHER

Photographs by Herbie Knott

SIDGWICK & JACKSON

LONDON

First published in Great Britain in 1983 by Sidgwick & Jackson Limited

Text copyright © Carol Thatcher 1983

Photographs copyright © Herbie Knott/Rex Features 1983
unless otherwise stated

ISBN 0-283-99063-5 (softcover)
ISBN 0-283-99068-6 (hardback)

Cartoons research by Deborah Pownall

Printed in Great Britain by
The Garden City Press Limited, Letchworth, Hertfordshire SG6 1JS
for Sidgwick & Jackson Limited
1 Tavistock Chambers, Bloomsbury Way
London WC1A 2SG

Diary
of an
ELECTION

THE OPENING
ROUNDS

Tuesday, 10 May
12.40 a.m.: Sound asleep in a hotel room in Hobart, Tasmania, I was woken up by the telephone ringing. 'Your mother has just announced that the election is on 9 June,' the voice of my editor, Margaret Willes, echoed over the trans-continental telephone system.

She was calling from Sidgwick & Jackson in London to discuss this diary, which we had already talked about in concept before I left England for Australia, some four weeks before, to write some stories for the *Daily Telegraph*.

I recall my reaction to her news being a four-letter word. It expressed my frustration at being twelve thousand miles away – in fact, about as far away as possible – from the scene of the action. My emotions were muddled between amazement at hearing that the balloon had gone up, and horror at having my slumbers interrupted with such a bombshell.

Some five hours before Margaret's call, at 8.40 a.m. Monday, London time, the morning after the Chequers' summit and just before the Prime Minister made the election announcement, I had telephoned Number Ten Downing Street to tell Mum that, owing to having been sent to Tasmania on a story, I would be back home a week later.

'How was the summit?' I asked her, well aware that Mum is the most security-conscious person on the phone and always gives only very cagey answers to questions. She said that it had lasted a long time, with 'a lot of methodical arrangements to be made' – a clear clue to June, but I still didn't anticipate a 9 June announcement.

We chatted about various problems associated with a flat which I was trying to buy. Mum is remarkable in the way in which she can switch from major international or political matters to minute domestic details within ten seconds. Although she ended the call with 'finish the *Daily Telegraph* story as quickly as possible', I didn't guess that she was sitting on such a momentous secret.

After Margaret Willes had finished her call, I tried to go back to sleep, but the thought kept turning over in my mind that my position had exploded the myth that a Prime Minister's children have advanced or inside information on election dates.

6.30 a.m.: Woken up again. This time it was Mum, on the line from Number Ten. 'I don't know if you've heard,' she began.

The Standard, 9 May

" Just as well we didn't print the Thatcher diaries, the election date was wrong ! "

London Express Service/The Standard

'Yes,' I interrupted, and lobbed in: 'Why now?'

The gist of her reply was the one that she gave everyone – about uncertainty and speculation. She added that certain international investments weren't being made in Britain because the perpetual state of election jitters was scaring off the prospective investors, which was bad for the country, the economy and the pound.

'I hope I get my flat, in case you need Flood Street back,' I said*, harking back to my purchase problems of our earlier conversation.

'I have no intention of needing Flood Street back,' she responded, sounding both buoyant and pragmatic.

This was all in sharp contrast to the kick-off to the previous election campaign. I remembered the March day in 1979 when Alison Ward, Mum's constituency secretary at the time, had called my Sydney home at 7.20 in the morning, shrieking down the phone: 'Your mother wants to tell you herself, but we won.' It was moments after Callaghan's Government had been defeated in a vote of censure in the House of Commons – the first time a Government had been defeated in exactly this way since 1841. All the drama in the division lobbies, the sensational result and the jubilation had come across in her voice.

On a lousy line, Mum kept saying, 'We won by one', which I heard as, 'We won, we won'.

'By how many?' I kept asking till at last I twigged, whereupon we continued. I was horrified that she had scraped in by the tiniest margin of one, she, on the other hand, was ecstatic that they'd *got* the vital one.

Back to the present. After a night dominated by phone calls and thoughts about the election ahead, I flew in a twelve-seater plane down to the remote south-west of the island, to look at the area of the proposed controversial Gordon-below-Franklin dam on which I had been assigned to do a story.

'How d'you think she'll go in the election?' the pilot asked me as I sat in the co-pilot's seat reading the election story on the front page of *The Australian*.

'I think she'll win,' I answered and realized that I hadn't

---

* Flood Street is my parents' private house in Chelsea, where they'd go if she lost the election. I'd been living there while flat hunting.

yet thought much about the election, let alone the result.

Back at Hobart Airport that night, as I walked across the tarmac admiring the pink sunset, that pilot was the first of many well-wishers who shouted out: 'Say good luck to your Mum for the election.'

I called back, 'Thanks'.

Canvassing in Finchley, the hustings, opinion polls and the whole works still seemed a world away.

I finished my assignment in Tasmania and, via Sydney, flew back to London. On the Tube from Heathrow to South Kensington, I read my neighbour's newspaper over his shoulder. The opinion poll percentages which gave the Conservatives a twenty-one per cent lead leapt out of the headlines – it was Friday, 13 May and twenty-eight days before that figure could be translated into results.

Friday, 13 May

I intended to get down to Chequers in time for a late lunch with Mum and Dad. Mum had been fulfilling a morning engagement at Euston Station where she named a railway engine after Airey Neave, her close friend and colleague who had been killed by an INLA bomb as he drove out of the House of Commons' underground car park four years before.

But my plan came unstuck when I discovered that my car insurance had expired during my five weeks in Australia, and I had to race up to the Automobile Association in Leicester Square and take out temporary cover. So it was not until three in the afternoon that I eventually swung through the side entrance at Chequers to a tranquil, uncampaign-like scene – the calm before the hectic three weeks ahead.

Mum, as usual on a Saturday afternoon, was ploughing her way through the piles of paperwork which arrive in the official red boxes. The red boxes are literally that, official box-like locked briefcases containing stacks of files, which are sent down from the Prime Minister's Number Ten office to Chequers at weekends, and which Mum works through in the flat, often very late at night, during the week. I popped my head round the door to say, 'Hello, I'm back from Oz,' and then went outside to see Dad, who was practising his golf

Daily Mail, 12 May

'Some of Saatchi and Saatchi's ideas are playing havoc with poor Denis's handicap.'

Associated Newspapers/Daily Mail

shots, although his chances of actually driving down a fairway in the foreseeable future seemed absolutely zero.

His improvised 'pitch and put' patch enjoys an imposing position, bang in front of the grand façade of the Buckinghamshire country mansion which Lord Lee of Fareham gave to the nation in 1918 for use as the Prime Minister's official country residence, and at the end of Victory drive, flanked by trees which were a gift from Sir Winston Churchill.

We chatted about the election timing. I was still surprised that Mum had chosen to go early, influenced perhaps by having been in Australia and seeing Malcolm Fraser's experience – he had opted for an early poll and been soundly defeated.

Dad said, taking another swing, 'I became a Juner after the horses had bolted with the carriages.' This was his way of saying that the speculation, in his opinion, made it virtually impossible not to choose the June option.

Somehow it seemed as though TINA – There is No Alternative – the acronym with which Mum was dubbed when she refused to vary her resolute approach in the days when the going was really rough, seemed to say something about her choice of polling day too. Later, she said that had she not gone for a June polling day but had delayed until October, or the following May, it would have meant almost non-stop electioneering, perhaps for months – a very un-healthy as well as undesirable state of affairs for every-one.

At tea, we talked about mundane details, such as hair appointments during the campaign, how our flat would function, food and drink arrangements and so on. During Mum's time, the flat at Number Ten Downing Street has never had a cook or housekeeper.

'Did she want someone now?' I asked.

'No, the one thing you're not short of during a campaign is food, everyone presses it on you,' she emphasized.

We didn't talk much about politics, there was going to be endless amounts of that to come. And anyway, campaigns seem always to have the same ingredients – smears, scares, and banana skins.

7.30 p.m.: Ron Thurlow, Chairman of the Finchley Conserva-tive Association, Andrew Thomson, Mum's agent, and Joy Robilliard, her constituency secretary, who formerly worked for Airey Neave, arrived for dinner to work out the Finchley campaign, appearances, walkabouts and so on. Not all of Mum's constituents, it appeared, expected to see their Conservative candidate.

Ron told how two of them, who had seen a 'Mrs Thatcher flies to Perth' newspaper headline – when Mum had gone up to the Scottish Conference on the previous Friday – had asked him, 'Will Mrs Thatcher be back from Australia in time to come to Finchley during the election?'

After supper Mum became immersed in discussions about leaflets, budgets, adoption meetings, her election address and canvassing arrangements. We all crawled around the floor re-arranging black and white photographs of her for a broadsheet to be titled 'The Finchley Leader', which was part of her campaign literature.

11.30 p.m.: Having given me strict instructions not to keep Mum up, Ron, Andrew and Joy left us.

The evening seemed a microcosm of the roles Mum would have to play in the coming weeks: candidate for Finchley, Leader of the Conservative Party, Prime Minister.

Dad went to bed and I went off in search of her glasses in the study. Goggles located, I left her reading through the campaign guide, promising that she wouldn't stay up all night.

My weekend was spent recovering from jet-lag and generally trying to acclimatize myself to the new atmosphere of the political campaign trail.

Monday, 16 May
After a day's work at the *Daily Telegraph*, and having been home to collect my car, I arrived at Number Ten just before eight to help dish out the supper.

I parked my three-year-old lime-green Ford Fiesta, which is notorious around Downing Street for its breakdown record – I am frequently having to recruit people to push start it – outside the front door. I greeted the policeman and the custodians who man the front door of Number Ten – no one has a key to it, there isn't a keyhole, just someone there twenty-four hours a day to let people in.

Once inside, I took the lift straight up to the second floor and walked along to our flat. There are several ways of getting up there: in the lift; or via the main staircase and past the first floor state reception rooms and the Prime Minister's study, and up a short flight of stairs. Mum has one of the world's shortest commutes, it is only seconds from the end of her bed to her desk. Then there are various other ways up to the flat via the backstairs and a veritable rabbit warren of passages. I once went downstairs to borrow some milk and found myself totally lost.

Number Ten looks deceptively small from the outside.

Behind that modest terraced façade, which has been the Prime Minister's official residence since 1735, there are sixty rooms, three staircases and offices for one hundred and forty people.

In the olden days, when governing the country was a rather more laid-back occupation, Number Ten was described by an official as 'a gentleman's home in which a little government takes place from time to time'. That has all changed. Today, Number Ten is offices over which the Prime Minister has a self-contained flat, converted out of attic rooms in the 1930s by Mrs Neville Chamberlain.

The flat is at the back of the house, overlooking Horse Guards Parade. Its layout resembles an extended railway carriage. Off a longish corridor lead a main bedroom and bathroom, sitting room, Mum's dressing room, a bathroom, Mark's bedroom and bathroom, Dad's study, spare-room-cum-my-room and bathroom. At the end there is a room which is used by Joy Robilliard as an office. On the other side of the corridor there's a laundry, and at the bottom of four or five steps, a small galley kitchen and an unimposing dining room for a squashed eight.

The flat is furnished quite ordinarily with Government furniture. Thus each incumbent doesn't have to move much in – a practical bonus, because defeated prime ministers, in common with detected Russian spies, have to be prepared to move out in a hurry.

The Prime Minister pays a service charge for living in the flat, which basically boils down to living fairly modestly over the shop. This is contrary to the popular image people have of grand living in Number Ten with hot and cold running footmen under the chandeliers.

The domestic arrangements are up to each individual Prime Minister. We have no live-in help, nor a housekeeper or cook. We have two wonderful dailies – Mossie and Edwina – who come in in the mornings and at weekends if Mum is around.

Our food and drink arrangements are haphazard, sometimes degenerating into chaotic. Mossie, Joy and I all do some of the shopping, and we have a freezer. Some people who come for what they anticipate will be a civilized drink with the

Prime Minister are mildly astonished to find her alone in the flat, dashing around trying to coordinate glasses, ice cubes, lemon, the gin and the tonic. But that's the way it is.

Food can be a problem. Mum doesn't give actual dinner parties, but occasionally colleagues or speechwriters qualify for supper if there is a working evening in the flat. Usually on these evenings Joy, Crawfie – David Wolfson's* secretary – or I try to be around, but sometimes Mum has to manage the operation on her own.

One MP was so horrified at this arrangement and, in particular, by the fact that his train of thought and the Prime Minister's attention kept being distracted by the bobbing up and down like a jack-in-the-box to check that nothing drastic had happened to the simmering frozen peas, that he read the Riot Act to her.

Mum decided to solve the problem by getting the girl who does the office lunches downstairs to make loads of easy 'shove in the oven to heat up' dishes for the freezer. Net result: one regular supper guest refused to come unless she varied the menu from the ubiquitous shepherd's pie which he'd had on about the previous three occasions in our flat.

That night it was only family supper. Mark and Dad were in the sitting room having a drink, and we were soon joined by Mum, from her study, who sank into an armchair with a weak whisky and soda – her favourite tipple.

Problem Number One: She hadn't managed to precis her election address – which is printed on leaflets and distributed to her constituents – down to the maximum 350 words and would have to have another go at it after supper.

Problem Number Two: Someone whom she had asked to take up a pair of curtains by four inches had chopped off the bottom by four inches.

I failed to see the drama, but apparently, if you know anything at all about curtains, it is an absolute 'no-no' to cut them off, you always take them up.

Mum went on for fifteen seconds in disbelief, admitting, with red boxes piled up awaiting her attention and an election campaign about to start, that curtain lengths – turned up or chopped off – were the least of her worries. So we established

* David Wolfson is head of Mum's political staff.

that an election address had to be chopped, but the curtains shouldn't be.

After our drinks, we went down to the dining room for a cold supper. Some of it Mum had brought back from Chequers the day before, considerably alleviating the catering crisis at Number Ten. Chequers has a staff and a chef, so there are no food traumas there. Quite the reverse in fact, the Prime Minister's official country residence not only runs like clockwork but has excellent food as well.

I accused Mum over supper of leaking information to a Sunday tabloid, which had described her as 'fanatically tidy', and Mark and me as 'fanatically messy'. She denied the leak but thought that the assessment was spot on.

We talked about various aspects of the campaign before Dad left for 'twenty-four hours off' at Scotney – the flat which we rent in a National Trust house in Kent.

Meals, if Mum has her way, never take very long. For a start, she has always eaten terribly quickly, and regards mealtimes as interruptions to getting on with more work, and so keeps them down to minimum length. Mark vanished downstairs to watch the news on the telly, which Mum knew she was on. She detests watching herself on the box and won't have it switched on until she is sure she is off.

I washed up and made coffee for us both.

Part of my job as Mum's dogsbody during the election campaign will be the duties of wardrobe mistress. So we started my briefing with a conducted tour of the relevant clothes, which she had arranged in the spare room cupboards.

Cupboard 1: A selection of navy and black suits. 'I am expected to look executive,' she explained, one of her meticulous principles on how to dress for the job.

I tried to memorize which blouse went under which suit. Then we went on to footwear. 'Shoes; these are "clodhoppers" for walkabouts,' Mum announced, indicating racks of shoe-tree-filled shoes at the bottom of the cupboard.

Cupboard 2: 'Best shoes for speech-making, must be comfortable when standing to make a speech.' In front of me were neatly labelled boxes containing different coloured suede court shoes.

Usually, she doesn't wear her best clothes on the campaign trail because they aren't enhanced by missiles of flour, eggs, tomatoes and so on.

Cupboard 3: 'Best cupboard, telly clothes,' those whose colour and style look good on the screen.

Mum nicknames her clothes, which is the only way of identifying them. 'Aubergine' (purple suit), 'Plum lightning' (patterned with red flashes), 'Cloudy' (white squirls on black), 'English garden' (herbaceous-border-coloured pattern).

Sometimes, we came across two that were alike, 'We got a job lot of material,' she'd explain.

Cupboard 4: On to dresses for evenings and rallies. 'Domino best' (chequerboard pattern with frilled collar), 'Domino simple' (the less glamorous version).

'Navy spot.'

'We've had one of those,' I chipped in.

'No, this is navy chiffon spot, see, see-through. That's navy *silk* spot.'

I'm guaranteed to get that wrong I suspect.

Even though there will be only one overnight tour, in Scotland, she always takes a suitcase which must contain reserve day clothes, a change for evening, spare tights, spare shoes, evening shoes, scarf to protect hairdo from the rain, hairspray and various other things. In addition, her white box beauty case must go, plus her briefcase.

I developed a secret dread about her clothes, feeling sure that I'd never manage to co-ordinate the programme and the outfits. I could foresee the Prime Minister arriving in 'gold stars', a very glamorous blue dress splattered with gold motifs, and high heels, at some sheet metal works in the Midlands.

I ceased worrying – she has very sexy legs and the dress was very pretty, so it might gain votes on the shop floor.

Lesson over, I made more coffee, she settled down to work.

Just before I went, we searched around for a list of the rehearsals on Horse Guards Parade. This is the time of year for Trooping the Colour and Beating Retreat, and they rehearse at the crack of dawn, right outside her bedroom window. She must feel that pageantry and politics have conspired to do her out of a decent night's sleep for three weeks.

I left her alone in the flat, wished her 'good luck' for the manifesto launch on Wednesday, and walked down the main staircase, which was in darkness.

The walls are lined with the portraits of all the previous Prime Ministers, none of whom, this century, has won a second consecutive term. If Mum, on 9 June, was to become the first, she would have a hat-trick of records to her name: the 1979 defeat of the Callaghan Government in a vote of censure by a majority of one; Britain's first woman Prime Minister with the Conservative election victory on 3 May 1979; and the first PM of a Conservative Government to return to Downing Street without a break for a second term.

The historical precedent is against her, but Polling Day still seemed a long way off. So did the lights of the corridors of power, as I tried not to fall down the stairs in the dark.

Tuesday and Wednesday were to be quiet days as far as the campaign was concerned, so I spent these working at the Daily Telegraph. *But Wednesday was to see the launch of the Tory Manifesto, and then electioneering would really start in earnest. The first event on the calendar would be Mum's adoption as the Conservative candidate for Finchley and Friern Barnet – to take place on Thursday evening.*

Wednesday, 18 May

The Labour Party launched its manifesto two days ago, on 16 May, while the Conservatives issued theirs today. Contents apart, the two documents could hardly be more different in appearance.

The Labour Party Manifesto, entitled 'The New Hope for Britain', has a recycled-paper feel, and is yellow with a scrapbook appearance produced by three black and white photographs. Its title appears in red at the top, the subtitle, 'Think Positive, Think Labour', and the price of 60p likewise appear in red, at the bottom.

The Conservative Manifesto is a smaller, booklet-like number with a glossy white cover. The top half of the cover is taken up with the title, 'The Conservative Manifesto 1983', in black, and at the bottom appears the red, white and blue logo variously described as the Olympic flame with a blue rinse, and the cross section of a soft-serve ice cream. In fact, much research went into producing a symbol identifiable with the Conservative Party's image, and this flame-like one won. It is also patriotic, and a corner of the Union Jack. It costs 25p.

Labour promise in their Manifesto a public spending programme of £11.5 billion, a reduction in unemployment to below one million within five years, a pledge to take Britain out of the Common Market, and a commitment to unilateral nuclear disarmament. The Manifesto also contains provisions for extensive nationalization, re-nationalization, and more power to trade unions. The *Daily Mirror* called it 'Labour "kiss of life" plan for Britain', while *The Times*, in a savage leader, dubbed it 'When New Hope is No Hope'. If Labour were to win on this Manifesto, *The Times* declares: 'The atmosphere would be xenophobic, illiberal, syndicalist and confiscatory. This party promises the moon; but it would have to borrow the moon. Somebody else, as always, would have to pay. There is no "New Hope for Britain" in this document. There is no hope.'

The Conservative Manifesto has as its theme a continuation of the resolute approach. It spells out the achievements of the past four years and sets out its plans for a second term: 'The choice before the nation is stark: either to continue our present steadfast progress towards recovery, or to follow policies more extreme and more damaging than those ever put forward by any previous Opposition.'

The Manifesto promises greater freedom for union members by the provision of secret ballots to elect officials, more privatization and a pledge to dismantle the Greater London Council.

The Times' leader, entitled 'Some Way Still to Go', stated: 'This is a cautious manifesto, carefully worded to see that it threatens nobody with a radical cutting edge, while asserting in moderate language the underlying principles which have inspired this Government's efforts to change direction.'

One thing that is certain about both these documents, and the manifestos of all the other parties too, is that every line will be attacked by opponents during the next three weeks; on television, radio, in newspapers, and on the stump.

WEEK ONE

Thursday, 19 May

Although it is eleven days since the announcement that polling day will be on 9 June, Mum doesn't officially start campaigning until tomorrow.

The consensus has been strongly that the best plan, this time, is to start late and to build up to a crescendo, instead of going off with an early bang and then getting forgotten, boring everyone stiff or flagging after a week or two.

This morning, Mum did a photocall and gave interviews to the press to show off the new bus, which will be her office-cum-campaign headquarters on the road.

Tessa Gaisman, a secretary in the political office downstairs in Number Ten, who will alternate with Alison Ward on the bus, found the experience an uncomfortable one. Sitting at one of the two desks in the office section at the rear of the bus, she was absolutely dreading Mum asking her either to type or to answer the phone. Usually Tessa is practically panic-proof and a model of efficiency, but she hadn't had time to read the instructions on how to operate the electronic, as opposed to electric, typewriter, and couldn't even have turned the thing on.

The radio telephone refused to function because, as the bus circuited Smith Square, it was surrounded by high buildings – Transport House, the nerve centre of the Labour Party, for one.

I arrived at Number Ten at about six in the evening to find Mum boiling the kettle in the kitchen to make herself hot lemon and honey. She wanted to fortify her voice, which was

Daily Telegraph, 20 May

Patrick Garland/Daily Telegraph

only just recovering from an awful cold, for her adoption speech in Finchley in one hour's time.

This will be her eighth election in the North London constituency of Finchley and Friern Barnet, the seat that she first won in 1959. In addition to her usual opponents, there are a bizarre selection of candidates campaigning for various obscure causes: Anthony Joseph Noonan (Ban Every Licensing Law); Laurence Gregory Spigel (Labour); Lord David Edward Sutch (Official Monster Raving Loony); Benjamin Collingham Wedmore (Belgrano Bloodhunger); Helen Mary Anscomb (Rail Not Motorway); Jane Joachim (Liberal/SDP Alliance); Brian Clifford Wareham (Party of Associates with Licensees); David Alec Webb (Anti-Censorship/Reform); Simone Joan Wilkinson (Women-Life, Earth/Ecology Party); and Anthony Peter Whitehead (Law and Order in Gotham City).

Joy Robilliard and I went up to Finchley in my car. We were the fourth car in the official convoy, and sat with the engine revving outside Number Ten ready for the off.

In a flash, the Prime Minister swept out of the front door and straight into the back seat of her car, which had its engine running too. The door slammed and it moved swiftly off. Instantly, the back-up car containing the garden room girl* followed, and so did Mark, who was hitching a lift with his security men.

I fell in behind them in a start which to me resembled a formula one car leaving the grid.

We swung into Whitehall and were away. Driving in a fast-moving convoy is a gruelling experience. I attempted to stay dangerously close to the bumper of Number Three car as it wove in and out of the rush-hour traffic in Park Lane. As it was a police car incognito, it could wave a little sign which read 'POLICE' at anyone who was a bit slow in moving aside. Obviously I had no such sign, but made a mental note that if I was going to have to do much of this agile motor-racing around town, which is much more Mark's scene than mine, I'd get one printed to read 'ME TOO'. I could then press it to the window when following an aggressively-driven police car displaying 'POLICE'.

Joy was very calm. I'd have been cowering under the dashboard by then if anyone drove me like that.

On arrival at the hall in Finchley, which was crowded and lit by television lights, we were conducted onto the platform. I had totally forgotten what it is like to sit on a platform staring into five television lights, and at rows and rows of people with press cameras clicking away *en masse*.

Mum was proposed as 'the best hope for Britain' and rose to start her fifty-minute speech. Determined and authoritative, she hammered home the achievements of the last four years:

> We have brought down the rate of inflation to less than five per cent and going down, the lowest rate for fifteen years.
> We have brought down interest rates.
> The strikes which gave British industry such a dismal

---

* This is the name given to the twelve Government (Civil Service) secretaries who work in the room adjoining the garden that Number Ten shares with Number Eleven Downing Street.

reputation are far fewer and mostly confined to the public sector.

We have brought down tax rates for managers and workers alike.

We have slashed the National Insurance Surcharge – Labour's tax on jobs – giving £2,000 million back to industry.

She launched a strong attack on Labour on the very subject which it had been predicted would be her Party's Achilles' heel – unemployment. 'Now, let's look at Labour's record,' she challenged, and got stuck in:

> Let them try and find a single Labour Government since the war which has left office with unemployment lower than when they came in.
> There isn't one.
> When Labour's present Leader was Secretary of State for Employment, in two short years unemployment doubled from 618,000 to 1,284,000. He did not have a magic formula then and he has not got one now. Mr Chairman, every Labour Government has promised to reduce unemployment, and every Labour Government has in fact increased it. And if ever there were to be another Labour Government, the same thing would happen again.

'Here Heres', applause and cheers filled the room.

We stood for the National Anthem and then, to the strains of a rather over-amplified rendition of *Land of Hope and Glory*, walked down through the body of the hall.

Mum radiated confidence, beaming at the loyal and warm reception she got from members of the audience, many of whom she obviously knew well.

Camera crews walked backwards filming her, their lights having already created something of a hothouse atmosphere during the past couple of hours. Mum squeezed along the crowded aisles and reached down the rows shaking hands, thanking people for their congratulations, and good wishes, and waving at supporters who were out of reach.

Back at Number Ten, she reflected that it had been hard to make people clap because they tend to freeze when the television cameras are there. Dad assured her that she had been terrific. She proceeded to get down to yet more work, but not before she had telephoned constituency Chairman, Ron Thurlow, to thank him and say how pleased she was at the way the meeting had gone.

We started to think about clothes for her trip to Cornwall the following day. This included going through several headscarves before we found one that would do.

Mum is meticulous, it must match, not be red – the Labour Party colour – and not have a foreign name or 'Made in Somewhere Overseas' emblazoned too conspicuously down the side. When your election address includes the maxim 'British is Best' and the press even inspect the tyres on the campaign bus to ascertain whether they are British or French retreads, you can't then appear as a walking ad' for our foreign competitors.

Friday, 20 May
My first thought on waking up in Number Ten was not to leave behind the Prime Ministerial wellington boots, mackintosh or hairspray.

This was the day that the Thatcher show got on the road, our inaugural fly awayday return to the West Country, and something of a test mission for the ones to come. Our itinerary was very much an early-in-the-campaign-type schedule – no major speeches or rallies, nothing too arduous. In fact, on paper it looked a very pleasant half day outing down to Cornwall and back in time for dinner. The territory used to be a Liberal stronghold until the Conservative candidate, Gerry Neale, won the seat of North Cornwall from the Liberal, John Pardoe, at the last General Election.

Mum left the flat at about 8.00 a.m. for the briefing of the Chairman, Cecil Parkinson, at Conservative Central Office in Smith Square. This was followed by the daily news conference and any other media interviews, before departure by plane, train, helicopter or road to that day's campaign destination. That, basically, is the blueprint for the days ahead.

26

Once she had left the flat, I packed her wellington boots – mine on loan as she had left hers down at Chequers – spare clothes in case she got terribly wet or muddy, or had something thrown at her, extra tights, and her beauty case.

10.30 a.m.: I left Number Ten for Central Office with one of the garden room girls. Even though it is election time, a garden room girl has to travel with the Prime Minister's party, and the official car has to follow the campaign bus in case there is a crisis which necessitates the Prime Minister attending to Government business, or returning quickly to London.

I met Alison Ward at Central Office. She is Mum's former constituency secretary who has been working for the Party Treasurer, Alistair MacAlpine, but who has come back to help out in the political office during the campaign. She is an absolute whirlwind of efficiency.

At Central Office, Sir John Eden, the former Member for Bournemouth, who isn't standing this time, is running the Prime Minister's office.

10.45 a.m.: Roger Boaden ordered everyone into a convoy of cars and we left for Victoria Station. There, we boarded the train for Gatwick and settled down in three reserved first-class compartments.

The party consisted of campaign manager and tour organizer, Roger Boaden, the man in charge of the programme, and of making it happen. Basically, where we go, what we visit, and the planes, trains, helicopters, buses and cars that are used, are all Roger's department.

Where politicians in other countries have small armies of advance men, aides and flunkies to get their campaigns on the road, in our case almost everything is done by an indefatigable trio – Roger plus his two secretaries.

This is the fifth time he's masterminded the campaign, and he celebrates quarter of a century with the Tory Party during the course of this current campaign – on 2 June, or what in his jargon is termed D minus 7.

Roger is virtually unflappable, with a talent for producing hitch-proof logistics. If you get left behind, it's likely to be the fault of Roger's hyper-efficiency rather than a cock up. It was probably due to the fact that you failed to get into your car in the motorcade in the five and a half seconds allocated, rather than the fact that the transport didn't turn up.

David Wolfson was another member of the party. So too was Ian Gow, MP for Eastbourne and Mum's Parliamentary Private Secretary, a post he has held for years. He will alternate on the tours with Michael Spicer, MP for Worcestershire South and Deputy Chairman of the Conservative Party.

The 'new boy' on the team is John Whittingdale, head of the political section of the Conservative Research Department. Described in *The Times* by the rather uncomplimentary soubriquet of 'cheapskate back-up', John, who is aged only twenty-three, is the campaign's one-man-think-tank and a mine of political and statistical information.

He first joined the Research Department as a library boy to fill in time before he went to University College at London University to study his first love – astronomy. Bitten by the political bug, he quit astronomy after six weeks and re-applied to read economics, returning to the Research Department to help with the 1979 General Election.

Now, with an economics degree to his name, he is back at Research. He arrived at the train today staggering under the weight of two massive suitcases, which would have notched up a hefty bill for excess luggage had they been summoned onto the airport scales. They turned out to be John's personal portable research library, into which he can delve for any fact needed as ammunition against the other side.

Suitcase Number One, from which John refuses ever to be separated, contains essential briefing material, such as the *Campaign Guide 1983*, current briefing, enough statistics to send the average computer into overdrive, files on difficult issues from the day's press conference, a 'dirty tricks' folder of nasty quotes from the other side, and all the parties' manifestos, including that of the Communist Party.

Suitcase Number Two is stacked full of further reading matter for the political expert – campaign guides dating back to 1974, manifesto briefings, biographies of candidates, and so on.

If asked, for instance, in a country area, about sows and

The Times, 10 May

'My specialist subject is British Prime Ministers, 1979–1988.'
© *The Times*

piglets, John would have before you in a flash a copy of 'The
Pig Industry Levy Bill' brief which, among other things, makes
compensation provisions for pigs with Aujeszky's Disease.

John relishes advanced queries with the kind of attitude a
Mastermind finalist adopts towards questions on his specialist
subject.

Today's party was completed by Dad, two security men,
and myself.

On the way, I got Mum, who was reading the papers, to try
on my boots – which fortunately fitted.

On arrival at Gatwick, Mum and Dad transferred to a car
and the rest of the party clambered aboard a mini-bus for the
short journey across the tarmac to the bottom of the plane's
steps. The plane the party had chartered from British Island
Airways, a BAC 1–11, was called 'Island Endeavour'. We will
be using it, or a twelve-seater helicopter from Battersea
Heliport, for all fly awayday returns.

Mum and Dad were much filmed as they went aboard but
once they were settled down in their seats, an agitated Derek
Howe (in charge of the press) announced that the airport
security hadn't let the stills photographers out to snap away at

29

the Prime Minister and husband getting on the plane. Now released, they had requested a re-run of the exercise.

Mum and Dad agreed, got off, posed for photographers on the steps, and got back on again. Returning to her seat, Mum observed, 'Strange to be asked for an encore before you start.'

'On behalf of British Island Airways and the Conservative Party, we welcome you on board . . .', the usual safety patter followed and we took off.

It was a fantastic flight with very pampered in-flight cabin service, no plastic, drinks out of crystal glasses and a cold salmon salad lunch.

With a pilot at the controls who didn't believe in hanging about, and tailwinds, we landed at St Mawgan in Cornwall half an hour ahead of schedule. Timing is crucial on a campaign. Too early, and the people who are meant to meet you might not have turned up or have got themselves organized; too late, and your supporters might have given up hope and headed off home.

Once off the plane, we boarded the specially-fitted-out bus which will be Mum's mobile office and campaign HQ for the next few weeks. To fill in time, she gave an interview in the back of the bus to the elder statesman of American television newsreaders, Walter Cronkite, who was filming for 'World In Action'.

Then at last we got on the road and made way to our first stop – a walkabout on the quay at picture-postcard Padstow, land of lobsters, fishing boats and Cornish quaintness.

As we approached, we heard on the radio a message from the local police which informed us that there was a crowd of about a hundred people, 'apparently friendly'.

Mum, who is an enthusiastic and experienced campaigner, jumped off the bus and plunged into the mêlée, shaking hands, asking questions, answering them, accepting good wishes from supporters and generally doing what is known in political jargon as 'pressing the flesh'.

Such walkabouts are stage managed by Roger Boaden, who tries to keep a semblance of order, aided by uniformed local police, Mum's security and Derek Howe, who controls a small army – over fifty this day – of photographers, television crews and journalists.

On the inside looking out, the fray passed in a blur of humanity. Overhead, we could see children on shoulders or held aloft, policemen's hats, and the boom mikes – extended pieces of audio equipment waved by television soundmen vaguely in the direction of the VIP's voice. At eye level, the world was just a sea of faces and the crush a cross between a rugger scrum and a Tube train in rush hour.

The press meanwhile recorded the scene for television viewers and newspaper readers from almost any vantage point which afforded them an aerial view. Today, these included the caterpillar wheels of a strategically parked crane, and piles of upturned fish crates.

In fact, in Padstow, Mum had competition for the day's star billing from the personalities behind some of the most famous by-lines in Fleet Street. 'It's her, it's her,' chorused a group of fans. But it wasn't Maggie who was the object of their adoring attentions, but the *Daily Express*'s star columnist, Jean Rook. Fresh from penning profiles of the world's superstars, she was following Mum on the campaign trail for a day.

Max Hastings, of Falklands fame, made one old military man's day when he signed an autograph for him. The Falklands factor was very much in evidence in the following press corps. Several of the reporters, photographers and cameramen who, a year ago, were eight thousand miles away in the South Atlantic covering the conflict, were now assigned to follow the lady whose war it very much was, as she makes a bid to get re-elected.

Two locals in the quayside crowd feared that the Iron Lady's presence in this sleepy port might prove provocative. 'Look, the Russians are coming now,' I overheard one say to another as the sound of low-flying aircraft came closer.

Ian Gow hopped off the bus with glee when he spotted the opposition, and proceeded to engage the local Socialist candidate, James Hayday, who was already being given a hard time by a vocal local, in a spirited debate.

The seat of Padstow is far from being a Labour stronghold; every Socialist candidate except one has lost his deposit in this constituency, and Mr Hayday was understandably coy about predicting his percentage of the vote on 9 June.

I asked another man, boasting an orange rosette, why he

was carrying round a colourful and splendid Indian head-dress, which seemed to be an incongruous addition to a candidate's props. It wasn't, he claimed defensively. It symbolized America's extermination of the Indians, which was what they would like to do to us with bombs given half a chance. Well, the thing about being on the election trail is that you encounter all points of view.

The programme said 'Depart Padstow 14.35 p.m.', so Mum was manoeuvred back into the bus and waved off by the last of the crowd.

David Wolfson had skipped the whole proceedings and, knowing the location of the local Cornish fudge shop as he has a holiday home nearby, had made a quick expedition into town and returned with a couple of bags of sticky melt-in-the-mouth goodies which we tucked into gratefully. That was in between directing Mum to wave at pockets of supporters and onlookers as we sped past. 'Wave, here on the right, coming up on the left on the pavement,' until David arbitrated, 'No, we only wave in marginals!'

Our next port of call was a two-hundred-acre dairy farm. The route to it involved negotiating several narrow winding lanes, which Roger had had measured in advance to make sure that our 8ft-6ins-wide bus would get through.

The visit to Trelyll Farm was why we had been given orders to bring wellington boots. Mum strode off at a furious pace with the owner, Mr Nightingale, to inspect some yonder silage field, hotly pursued by the press.

The scene was like something out of a 'Carry On' film, a kind of media and political circus amongst the cowpats. Some photographers and television cameramen, racing to round up on Mum for the perfect full-frontal rural shot, accidentally landed themselves straight in a quicksand-like smelly bog.

There were wails of horror from the equipment-laden lads, who included Martin Cleaver, MBE, of Falklands fame, whose award-winning shot of the *Antelope* had been splashed across the world's front pages. Halted by the commotion, the Prime Minister offered the muddy mob a rescuing hand from the safety of *terra firma*, while their press colleagues snapped and filmed the episode.

Two other reporters who were larking around, one taking a

photograph of the other attempting to interview a cow, notepad and pencil in hand, were slightly embarrassed when they turned round to find themselves being filmed by a television crew to provide an example of what journalists get up to when they are sent to cover an election campaign.

Mum posed on the steps of a farm vehicle which was towing a dangerous-looking piece of equipment, complete with blades and spikes. She visited the cowshed before having a cup of tea in the farmhouse, while the telly reporters did their stand-ups leaning against farm fences, and others hosed off their wellies.

It was then all back on the buses and on the road again for the last stop of the day.

When we arrived at a car park in Wadebridge, Mum was given an enthusiastic welcome by the large crowd waiting to see her. In the shadow of the freezer centre and squash courts, and under threatening clouds, she energetically campaigned, watched by a silent anti-nuclear demonstration.

Fleet Street observed this impromptu rally, balanced precariously on a bulldozer parked at one end of the car park. Mum then gave a short standard sort of electioneering speech from the loudspeaker van of the Conservative candidate, Gerry Neale, before being clapped back to the steps of the bus – a resounding success.

The campaign trail can seem a small world. At Padstow, Mum had met someone who had campaigned for her back in 1959, while in Wadebridge, John Whittingdale broke into a burst of spontaneous waving when he recognized his secretary's parents in the crowd.

Back on board the plane we were revived by a choice of Devon teas or sandwiches and champagne. But the day wasn't over for Mum, nor was the flight all relaxation. Jean Rook interviewed her for twenty minutes, and a camera crew came up to take in-flight shots, which meant Dad handing his glass of champagne back to me before the inevitable order from the camera man as he rolled the film, 'Talk naturally between yourselves.'

A member of the TV team said thank you and 'Enjoy the next two weeks.' 'Thank you,' replied Mum, 'and I hope to enjoy the following two weeks even more.' Roger Boaden then checked another day's travelling programme with her before we landed at Gatwick.

Back at Number Ten, she went through Finchley correspondence with Joy Robilliard, had supper, and then settled down to speechwriting for next week's rallies.

These are very much early days in the campaign, with a little sniping but no real getting to grips with the issues' dogfights.

Saturday, 21 May

The day had been planned as a candidate's morning in the constituency, shopping in a local supermarket and doing a walkabout canvassing the support of Saturday shoppers – about the most basic form of electioneering. Only in this case the reality was rather different. The constituency was Finchley and the candidate the Prime Minister. Budgen's supermarket in High Road, East Finchley, provided the stage for the drama.

At about 9.50 a.m. we arrived, and Mum, one foot on the pavement, was immediately immersed in a scene which could only be described as the Maggie and Media show. Cameramen and photographers, with all the determination of bargain hunters in Harrods' sale, lurched towards the entrance of the supermarket in a massed scuffle.

We came to rest halfway down an aisle and, because we had missed out the part where normal shoppers acquired a basket or a trolley, we had to wait until one could be brought to us. 'Basket coming,' a voice approximately mid-throng announced and, sure enough, like a lifebelt, it was rather gingerly lowered to the Prime Minister, who was trapped in the epicentre of the mêlée.

The media then had to be reshuffled, a manoeuvre that was accompanied by much cursing from those who had to surrender their close-up positions and to jockey again to somewhere from which they could reasonably hope to get a shot of the Downing Street shopper in action.

As Mum advanced, so the press walked backwards, considerably endangering the display pyramids of tins and packets, and threatening to demolish the whole egg stock.

Mum beguiling Mr Nightingale of Trelyll Farm during her
visit to North Cornwall. The outfit is completed by my wellies
to provide the 'Land Girl Thatcher' image, according to *The
Times*

Right: The best laid plans of mice and men . . . thirty days' rain and an ITN cameraman, weighed down by high technology ENG equipment, sinks into the Cornish mud. The Prime Minister, on *terra firma*, offers a rescuing hand

Below: Denis, 1979 campaign: 'If we don't look out, we'll have a dead calf on our hands . . .' (© Press Association) Denis, 1983 campaign: 'They look fairly well grown, that lot.'

A quiet moment amid the hubbub –
Mum and Dad relax on the campaign
plane. They were booked in as Mr
and Mrs Turnbull in seats 1A and B

How not to meet
eople . . . The
e Minister
tantly cocooned
her public. Apart
the press
ographers, only a
le of bemused
ish fishermen have
red a grandstand
. Meanwhile, in the
e were the following:
m; 2 Dad; 3 Ian
, Mum's
amentary Private
etary; 4 Gerry Neale,
candidate for North
wall; 5 Derek
e, press officer; 6
d Wolfson, chief of
n's political staff; 7
Witchell, BBC; 8
Rook, *Daily Express*;
rdon Shattock,
tern Area Chairman

The Lady
ishes. Mum bent
n suddenly, and the
way her position
d be located was by
ing at the anxious
ces of Denis and her
rity men

Doorstepping in her constituency of Finchley. 'I hope that I can count on your
support' – proverbial door-to-door canvassing, but grabbing a quiet moment is harder
for the Prime Minister than for most other
candidates

Right: The Labour Manifesto, 'The New Hope for Britain', comes in for some eagle-eyed scrutiny

Below: Speech-time on the campaign trail can mean saying a few words from the back of a horse-box in Castle Acre, Norfolk, or a major rally address with the trappings of pomp and autocue in Cardiff City Hall

Visitors to Harry Ramsden's Fish and Chip Restaurant in Leeds must have been horrified by the invasion of the Prime Ministerial party, quickly followed by the massed media. The official table got on with their fish and chip lunch, while Dad and I had more informal talks with some of the diners

Some photographers, with their obsession for high places, balanced on the edge of fish-finger-filled freezers, and one television cameraman took up a commanding position on the pinnacle of dozens of tins of Nesquick.

A vista to the dairy products section opened up to Mum, and I realized that shopping of this kind was an entirely new experience to her. She probably hadn't practised this thoroughly ordinary chore since she became Prime Minister. I foresaw that she was going to buy what she could reach rather than what we needed at Number Ten – loo paper and instant coffee – so I elected to go off and do the weekend shopping.

As the police wouldn't let any real live shoppers in until our charade had departed, I had the aisles to myself and whipped round in record time, paid and put the box of provisions in the back of the car.

I returned for the finale – the Prime Minister paying at the checkout. Mum waited while her purchases were totted up, and then came a hiccup.

'Carol, please come and pay,' requested the Iron Lady from the middle of the crush. Ducking under boom mikes and pushing through the solid wall of Nikon and Canon camera-carrying humanity I coughed up £11.94 and loaded Lymsewold, packeted ox tongue, light bulbs, ham and pâté into two carrier bags.

Mum, meanwhile, had dropped the housewife bit and got back on a political wavelength. As cassette tapes recorded and reporters scribbled, she held forth on food prices, inflation and Conservative policy on consumer issues.

The show over, we left Budgen's to return to being an averagely hectic Saturday morning suburban supermarket – a haven of peace and tranquillity in comparison.

The group that progressed up the High Road was a far from happy bunch of people. There was aggro at all levels: the Socialist supporters opposed Maggie; the public who wanted to meet the Prime Minister couldn't because, as they saw it, the Saturn-like rings of poisonous press surrounding her made it impossible, and they whinged; the stills photographers thought that the electronic cameramen were hogging the limelight; and the 'words' variety of the species objected to their picture-taking colleagues monopolizing the front line.

Two photographers showed initiative and appeared in first floor windows, showering us with cement filings and bird shit as they leant out to snap away.

Eventually, we took refuge in Chivers Brothers Motors, a motorist-cum-hardware shop, and kept the press out. Mum decided on the spot that Flood Street was in desperate need of a new hammer and screwdriver, bought them, and got me to pay. Very expensive things these elections, I thought to myself.

Backwards, sideways and, for the fortunate few, forwards, we stumbled across the pedestrian crossing and steered the Maggie/media mass towards Bryson's the printers. Here, Mum topped and tailed her election address, some sixty thousand copies of which were about to be printed.

She had about seven attempts with a felt-tipped pen at getting 'Dear Elector' right, and about eight at writing 'yours sincerely, Margaret Thatcher' exactly to scale. Eventually, she came about as near as any candidate has to cutting and pasting their own election address. She didn't want the printers to have to reduce her signature, and so measured the space into which it had to fit, cut it out, asked for a stool on which to sit to erase the wobbly effect you get when writing standing up, and finished the job – the pragmatic approach.

Mission accomplished, we set off to canvass house-to-house along several nearby residential roads. But this turned out not to be an overwhelming success. We had chosen an area which wasn't Conservative. Our task was made even harder by the fact that it was the morning before the Cup Final, so that many people were out getting their shopping organized, while others were reluctant to have the accompanying media invasion on their doorsteps.

By now, we had grown into quite a crowd. We wove along the pavement, crossed the road several times and covered three streets, finishing seconds before a violent hailstorm. This finally dampened our spirits, and we duly made off to the constituency campaign headquarters for meetings and lunch.

Mum was displeased about the morning's lack of organization, and said so. Why hadn't our loudspeaker been around? Why hadn't more workers been out locating supporters? She is a pro' and expects and demands professional standards from others. Elections and votes are won only if you work at it, she said emphatically, before getting down to work on constituency correspondence.

After lunch with Party workers, she visited an old people's home on the way back to Number Ten, where more work awaited her on the red boxes, the campaign and her speeches.

Saturdays are usually reserved for campaigning in Finchley, but the following weekend she will be in the United Stated, at Williamsburg for President Reagan's summit. The third and last Saturday will be a day of furious campaigning — the final run-up to Polling Day on Thursday, 9 June.

Sunday, 22 May

Conservative Shrimsley, chief of press and communications at Conservative Central Office, and Stephen Sherbourne, from the Conservative Research Department, arrived at Number Ten to brief Mum before she took part in an independent radio phone-in with Peter Allen at 11.00 a.m. They were joined by Gordon Reece, Mum's much publicized publicity consultant and so-called 'image builder', who had just flown in from Los Angeles. Gordon was head of publicity at Conservative Central Office during the 1979 election and now enjoys something of a high, rather flash, public profile. For the past three years he has been working for the head of Occidental Oil, Dr Armand Hammer, in California.

Installed in LBC's studios in Gough Square, Mum donned the headphones in her own inimitable way – with the top part round her neck so that her hair-do should not be disturbed. During the next hour on air, she fielded questions from callers around the country in the first of three phone-ins with party leaders.

Peter Allen started by saying that by far the largest number of questions and comments from those who wanted to talk to the Prime Minister involved the economy and unemployment.

James from Glasgow asked her to justify how she could spend £10 billion of taxpayers' money on Trident nuclear missiles, when there are basically four million unemployed in the country. Hadn't she got her priorities wrong?

No, I have not. The priority is to defend our way of life in this country and almost everyone, whether they're employed or unemployed, if I was to ask them what is the characteristic of this country, would say Britain is a free country.

The fact is that peace has been kept in Europe for thirty-eight years. Indeed, where we've had nuclear weapons there has been peace in spite of the fact that in the rest of the world there have been 140 conventional conflicts. What has happened is strong defence, including a balance of nuclear weapons, has kept peace in our country and in Europe.

James wasn't satisfied, and thought it a phenomenal amount of money which could be used more usefully to fund the National Health Service and new roads.

James, I must disagree with you. I do not think I could go along with a policy which says we abandon our independent nuclear deterrent while we leave colossal numbers, I think two thousand, strategic ballistic missiles in the hands of our sworn enemies. Enemies that didn't hesitate to go in and crush Hungary, Czechoslovakia and Afghanistan. It's weakness that attracts war, it's strength and balance that has given us peace.

Other calls came from places as diverse as Swansea, Islington, Cardiff, Beaconsfield, Bermondsey, Nottinghamshire and Bristol, and, apart from further points on unemployment and the economy, covered Northern Ireland, education, rate reform and capital punishment.

Mum and Gordon returned extremely pleased with the way the broadcast had gone: justifiably, as it had been a polished performance. Dad had gone off to Scotney for the day as Number Ten, and our flat in particular, is a claustrophobic place at weekends. Mum, Gordon, Mark and I drank champagne – in aid of Gordon, who is renowned for his taste for bubbly – and then had a quick lunch.

The perpetually effervescent Gordon suggested a newspaper advertisement with a picture of Michael Foot and the

caption, 'As a pensioner, he'd be better off under a Conservative Government'. Mum squashed that immediately, saying
no way, as it was below the belt.

Much of the rest of the day she worked solidly, with an
unquenchable capacity for the red boxes, speechwriting and
constituency correspondence.

Monday, 23 May
Our campaign day began at Battersea Heliport, where we all
assembled and boarded a twelve-seater helicopter for the
fifty-minute flight down to Bristol.

Our destination was a community centre and machine tool
factory near Bristol, and then we were to go on to a major rally
at Cardiff City Hall.

11.50 a.m.: We landed at British Aerospace, Filton, and
transferred to the campaign bus for the short drive to
Longwell Green Community Centre. This lies within the
constituency of Wansdyke, the eighty-fourth most marginal
seat as far as the Conservatives are concerned. It is named
after an ancient ditch and consists mainly of commuter
communities between Bristol and Bath.

The Socialist Workers' Party knew we were coming and
had positioned a handful of noisy protesters at the entrance,
chanting, 'Out, Out, Out'. Banners with motifs like 'Workers
Power not Nuclear Power' and 'Kick the Tories Out'
indicated their political preferences.

Mum left the bus and was immediately engulfed in the
crowd, and the media push-and-shove match. *Land of Hope and
Glory*, pouring out of the loudspeaker system, drowned the
noises of dissent from across the road.

Inside, Mum played with a children's playgroup, who
looked round wide-eyed as Fleet Street orchestrated their
playtime to get the best camera angles.

She then wished happy birthday to an old age pensioner
before, visibly moved and touched, presenting seven-year-old
leukaemia victim, Martin Whale, with a medal for bravery.

She declined to be photographed pulling a pint behind the
bar, even though ITN were already positioned on their

portable steps and photographers were poised along the bar to record the event. She explained later on the bus that had she obliged them, it would have been the photograph of the day and used by everyone. If they were going to use any shot, she wanted it to be one of Martin, to whom it would mean much more . . . .

Back on the bus, we moved on a short distance to a local factory, the machine tool manufacturers, Bristol Erickson, where we were scheduled to spend forty-five minutes. Demonstrators and supporters were both one step ahead of us so we arrived to the mixed sound effects of boos and cheers.

Mum was rapidly briefed by the management of Bristol Erickson on its work-force, production, technology and order book before touring office sections and the shop floor at a pace somewhere between a quick march and a jog.

In production control, looking at a computer screen of figures with her scientific, economic and Prime Ministerial eye for analysis, she asked about an order/delivery.

'It's overdue,' someone admitted.

'Oh, I'm sorry,' she apologized for having brought this fact to everyone's attention, and quickly and diplomatically substituted, 'Well, it's almost ready.'

She donned safety glasses to inspect some of the 180 machines on the shop floor. Noisy machines, some shaped like sub-machine guns, were turning, slicing through metal, oozing out shavings, and producing phallic forms.

Mum whipped round, totally and enthusiastically immersed, questioning their operators about what they did, how quickly, what happened to the end product and please could she have a go at the machine. At one machine, the button she pressed turned a toolholder in one minute forty seconds as she peered at it, fascinated, going through its cycle, and she was given the half-finished component, which had definite paper-weight potential.

Time to go, and we ran the gauntlet of the crowd with our eyes on the open door of our bus a few feet ahead. As we slowly manoeuvred out we were a sitting duck for every sort of reaction from the people outside. Supporters smiled, waved and cheered, blew kisses, gave us the thumbs-up sign, clicked instamatics and bobbed up and down excitedly holding Conservative posters aloft. The anti-Maggie mortals among them gave us the thumbs down and the two-fingered salute, jeered, booed, shouted, shook clenched fists and brandished hostile posters and banners. Mum moved from side to side in the bus acknowledging supporters and waving back.

Ahead of us was an hour-long drive to Cardiff. John, Alison, Tessa and Mum's security man played travelling Scrabble at the back of the bus. They built up QUAILS, VETO, MICE, WAXY and GRUBS on the board balanced on the back seat as the bus sped down the M4. Roger Boaden was on the radio telephone finalizing flight times to Manchester for a future rally and arranging details of other tours with Central Office.

Sir Ronald Millar, playwright, had joined us in Bristol to help with some final polishing on the night's rally speech. As we crossed the Severn Bridge, Mum was engrossed in familiarizing herself with the speech, making the odd amendment to the sixty-two-page script which she had already worked on late at night and for several evenings with Ferdinand Mount and other speechwriters. Ferdy Mount, as he is known, was appointed head of the Number Ten policy unit in April 1982. Ex Oxford, he used to write for *The Spectator*, and he has been speechwriter-in-chief of this campaign.

Mum and David Wolfson conferred in the front of the bus: 'Page thirty, change so and so, page fifty-one, cross out something else,' and in went a new phrase.

Baskets of flowers and posies lay on the seats, coats and raincoats were piled in the overhead racks and briefcases lay on the floor. We munched our way through packets of chocolate biscuits and consumed bitter lemon, tea and coffee out of paper cups.

We were able to spend two and a half hours at the Angel Hotel in Cardiff, before the Welsh Area Rally. No rest though if you're on an election trail. Mum was briefed for a television interview, did the interview, met local Conservative Party representatives to discuss which seats were potentially winnable, and to hear their progress reports.

More work was put into the speech in the bedroom, which was serving as an office. Alison and Tessa were working flat out, typing the speech onto Autocue tape for use in the same type of machine that President Reagan introduced to Britain when he used one during his address to a joint session of the Houses of Parliament two years ago.

Mum rehearsed with one under the direction of Harvey Thomas, a publicity consultant with Central Office who directed the Billy Graham crusades for fifteen years, and who is a public-speaking and Autocue expert. She quickly got the hang of the machine and used Autocue for the first time at the last Conservative Party Conference in Brighton.

The tape is run under two cameras backstage, which reproduce it on two monitors lying on their backs either side of the speaker's lectern. These reflect a reverse image of the text, which appears the right way round on two glass panes shaped like inward leaning music stands, placed at eye level to the right and left of the lectern. The operator, backstage in the wings or under the stage, turns the words to follow the speaker, varying the tempo to accommodate applause, cheers and ad libs.

We were opposite Cardiff Arms Park and a stone's throw from Cardiff Castle, but this was a campaign scene which could have been in any hotel in any city.

I told Mum how terrific she had been at Erickson's that afternoon, and she replied that the way to get a response was to put a colossal amount of effort into it. She is a tireless and energetic campaigner who never loses sight of the fact that the objective is to win votes and the only way to succeed is hard work. She was calm and confident about the speech. The best training for the campaign trail is four years as Prime Minister.

Having worked immensely hard every minute of those years, she knew her stuff back to front and had been used to being cross-examined on it across the despatch box in the twice-weekly Prime Minister's Question Time in the House of Commons.

Her mission between now and polling day is to sell the achievements of the last four years and to expose the Labour Party's Manifesto as the devastating document and extreme left-wing set of proposals it really is.

Her speech and the rally in the City Hall that night were a great success. She began by reminding the audience:

Four years ago, we launched our campaign in this great city in this same hall. I seem to remember we didn't do too badly . . . .

At that General Election, there were more Conservative MPs returned in Wales than in any election since the war. But in this Party we don't stand still. Last time, you gave us a cricket eleven to take to Westminster, this time we want to see a rugby fifteen – a Welsh rugby fifteen.

Later, she delivered the attack. Her target: page thirteen of the Labour Party Manifesto, 'The New Hope for Britain', the section entitled 'Finance for Industry'.

'Mr Chairman, I have here the Labour Party Manifesto,' she said, waving the yellow-covered 'The New Hope for Britain', of which the Conservative Party had bought five thousand copies.

I'm told that a member of Labour's Shadow Cabinet described it as 'the longest suicide note ever penned'.

I can tell you this: if the British people were to put their signature to it, it would be a suicide note for Britain too.

This document was written by the extreme Left. Labour hopes to goodness you won't read it [laughter].

They also hope you won't read the background documents, where they've revealed even more of the terrifying truth.

But if they ever got the chance, they'd claim they had a mandate to carry out every single one of the extreme measures in their Manifesto. It is important that Britain should know what Labour would do to Britain if they had the chance.

Let me tell you about it briefly, and I won't paraphrase it. I'll quote it directly.

First, nationalization, because you should know and everyone should know what they're proposing.

This is what they say, Labour 'will establish a significant public stake in electronics, pharmaceuticals, health equipment and building materials: and also in other important sectors as required in the national interest'. That's a start.

43

Labour will 'take powers to invest in individual companies, to purchase them outright, or to assume temporary control'.

And, of course, they'd re-nationalize everything that has been de-nationalized by this Government.

And how will they pay for this vast State grab? I'll tell you, it says in one of the background documents.

Well, they've got their eyes on your pension scheme and your life assurances.

Oh yes, you should know this. They will take your pension contributions and your life assurance premiums and spend them on their Socialist schemes. And there are eleven and a half million people who are members of occupational pension schemes. It's all here in their Manifesto and it confirms their Conference Statement, 'The Financial Institutions'.

They will set up, and I quote, a 'National Investment Bank'. 'We will', they say, 'expect the major clearing banks to co-operate with us fully in these reforms in the national interest. However, should they fail to do so, we (that is, them) shall stand ready to take one or more of the banks into public ownership [laughter and applause].'

Listen, this is deadly serious, this is why they hope you won't read it but everyone should know.

I am not putting words into their mouths. I am reading to you from the Manifesto.

'One or more'? Barclays? NatWest? Lloyds? Or the lot? It's a question of obey them to the letter or be nationalized. It's the language of the blackmailer through the ages.

The Labour Party goes in for nationalization like other people go in for stamp collecting; they want at least one of each – one of the big banks, one of the big pharmaceutical companies, one of the big electronics companies, one of the big building firms: Beechams, GEC, Plessey, Barratt, Taylor Woodrow; nobody could know who would be next.

Under a Labour government, there's virtually nowhere you could put your savings where they would be safe from the State.

44

They want your money for State Socialism and they would mean to get it if they got in.

Put your savings in the bank – and they'll nationalize it.

Put your savings in a pension fund or life assurance company – and a Labour Government would force them to invest the money in their own Socialist schemes.

Put your money in your socks and they'd nationalize socks. Mr Chairman, do people really want Labour to take charge of their savings? Let them answer with a resounding 'No' on 9 June.

After acknowledging the enthusiastic cheers from the audience and pausing to say goodbye in a nearby committee room, Mum and Dad left by car for London. The rest of the party returned by air to Gatwick, but Mum had elected to travel by car because the trip to the airport, the flight, and the journey back from Gatwick would have gained her only about twenty minutes, and a lot of hassle. Her driver, Ken, estimating the journey on the M4, added thoughtfully that if she nodded off, he'd slow up, so that she could use the dead time to get some sleep.

Tuesday, 24 May
Today, our fly awayday return consisted virtually of an extended lunch-break by the sea – without the leisure or recreation that such a junket implies.

We helicoptered down to Kent to spend three hours from noon to three o'clock in Deal and Dover. Setting off from Battersea Heliport, we flew down the River Thames over the Houses of Parliament, the Tower of London and the Thames Barrier, before landing half an hour later at the Royal Marine Depot in Deal. On the walk across the grounds to the campaign bus, Mum beetled off to chat up some firemen who were hovering on the perimeter. She is highly unpredictable on walkabouts. Heading in a clearly defined direction, she'll suddenly break into a trot when she spots a group of people to whom she wants to talk at the back of the crowd, on the opposite side of the street, or at the back of the hall, after which she has to be got back on course.

We were in Kent mainly to support candidate Peter Rees, whose constituency of Dover has suffered under the boundary changes. He has lost some of his Conservative areas to the new adjacent constituency of Thanet South. These additions have considerably helped neighbouring MP, Jonathan Aitken of TV AM fame. His potential majority has been increased to a hefty figure, leaving Peter Rees' seat looking a bit risky.

Our first stop was at Walmer Lifeboat Station, where Mum and Dad met the crew of the lifeboat and the Institute Committee. From one member of the committee, Cecil Prime, they heard about another waterborne operation. Mr Prime's son, John, had been the navigator on board HMS *Fearless* and had taken part in the landing at San Carlos Bay during the Falklands invasion. He has just been appointed Assistant Queen's Harbour Master in Port Stanley.

Togged up in an orange standard issue oilskin jacket, Mum cautiously ascended the ladder for her conducted tour of the lifeboat – in dry-dock. I winced as the stiff sea breeze demolished her hairdo. 'Exit Nationwide hair,' I thought to myself. I was relieved to find on the day's programme that, in fact, the rescuing services of hot curlers had been ordered for 4.00 p.m., before she left for the BBC to appear on 'Nationwide'.

Her glance across the Channel towards France must have been one of mixed feelings. Mitterand is not running the country in a way she would endorse, but at the same time, she is bashing Labour for its pledge to get us out of the Community, of which France is such an important part. With this paradox in mind, she returned to dry land. But, to the consternation of the photographers, she came down the aluminium ladder backwards – the safe option.

On rolled the campaign bus for this trip by the sea, to Deal Conservative Party offices where a charming caricature of a Tory lady introduced her workers to Mum and Dad as 'the old and the bold'. About sixteen of them were hard at it, addressing envelopes, consulting lists and getting election addresses in the mail. It could have been a scene out of *Anyone for Denis*.

So too could Dad's remarks on the bus as he waxed lyrical about the quality of the local golf courses. He was probably day dreaming of getting himself out of a bunker, rather than relishing the thought of the much tougher challenge of helping 'the Boss' give a hand to a candidate who was under some pressure in this golf-course-land seat.

On Dover promenade, we reached the nadir of press/Party relations. The photographers wanted Mum on the beach and them on the sea-wall, or *vice versa*; but no one told Mum that. There was much milling around in a situation which was unsatisfactory for everyone. Scouting around the back of the mêlée I fell over Dad, who was taking a position appropriate to a former rugger referee.

'I thought you were in the middle,' I said.

'No way, there's neither pleasure nor profit in this,' he retorted.

No doubt he was wishing that he could show the yellow card to a few of the Nikon-wearing, notepad-carrying players in front of him and send even more of them off. Not a champion of reptiles' rights, Dad.

Someone declared half-time and the players adjourned to the White Cliffs Hotel, while we went into the next-door Port of Dover's boardroom for a quick lunch.

David Wolfson appeared to expedite departure. He'd heard that Michael Foot was planning to make a statement in an attempt to paper over the cracks in his Party's defence policy and to reconcile the differences in Labour's non-nuclear policy between his deputy, Denis Healey, and what had been said in the Manifesto. Obviously, Mum had to read that before 'Nationwide'.

On the way back to the helicopter, we visited Dover Conservative Party offices where the campaign bus, resembling a huge beached whale, separated Conservative supporters and CND opponents, both trying to outshout the other.

Inside, Mum appeared at a first-floor window and made an abortive attempt to say a few words. This was later reported as having been halted by the demonstrators. Not so, the blame should have been placed on the pathetic amplification qualities of the loud hailer she was using, which rendered almost every word inaudible.

Back in Number Ten, Carmen curlers in her hair and a copy of Mr Foot's statement in her hand, she got ready for 'Nationwide'. She soon left with Gordon Reece for the BBC studios at Lime Grove to do the 'On the Spot' segment of the programme with Sue Lawley, answering questions put to her from viewers around the country.

The best way to describe what went on the air is that it represented an example of the most crass nastiness and discourtesy shown to a Prime Minister on a television programme. In thirty-five minutes there were only seven questions, and the programme was allowed to ramble on and on in an unattractive and unproductive fashion.

This was how one of the question-and-answer segments went:

Sue Lawley: Right, I want to move on. Let me bring in Bill Sykes from Crawley in Sussex. Mr Sykes, your question please?

Mr Sykes: Five years ago, Mrs Sally Oppenheim said that if the purchasing power of the pensioners' Christmas bonus is to be maintained, it should be £20. Last year, Lord Trefgarne said it needed to be about £35. It is still only £10, in spite of the TV licence increase of £21 which nullifies the Christmas bonus and leaves the pensioner £11 worse off.

Sue Lawley: What's the question Mr Sykes? You want some more money?

Mr Sykes: How can you call yourself a caring Government when you treat the pensioners so shabbily?

Sue Lawley: Mrs Thatcher, can I nag and ask for a brief answer.

Mrs Thatcher: Yes, I will give a brief answer. First, on your weekly pension. The weekly pension has gone up more than prices have gone up. Your last increase under the last Government was in November 1978, prices have risen since then by sixty-one per cent.

Mr Sykes (interrupting): Mrs Thatcher, I'm talking about the Christmas bonus . . .

Mrs Thatcher: But the pension has gone up by sixty-eight per cent. We have paid a Christmas bonus each and every year we have been in office, yes, it has only been £10. You did not get a Christmas bonus even of £10 for two years when Labour was in office . . .

Mr Sykes (interrupting): Labour doubled the pensioners' bonus from £5 to £10 . . .

Mrs Thatcher: You did not get a Christmas bonus for two years during the lifetime of the last Labour Government, they paid you nothing at all in respect of two years.

Sue Lawley: Do you remember that, Mr Sykes, in 1975 and 1976?

Mr Sykes: No.

Mrs Thatcher: We have paid one each year. It is on top of the National Insurance Pension. Again, money that goes out has to be met by money that comes in, this time from the taxpayer. And we have felt that, having kept the pension well ahead of prices – and it will still be well ahead of prices this November – we could not actually ask the taxpayer to pay more to add to the Christmas bonus.

Mr Sykes: I am talking about the Christmas bonus, Mrs Thatcher . . .

Mrs Thatcher: Yes, I have just answered about the Christmas bonus.

Mr Sykes: No, you haven't, you've avoided the question.

Mrs Thatcher: I'm sorry . . .

Mr Sykes: We're £11 worse off because of the increase in the TV licence from £25 to £46.

Mrs Thatcher: May I repeat, the television licence you'd expect to come in the normal cost of living, and it does come on the normal Retail Price Index. We have, in fact, kept the pension ahead of prices, the weekly pension . . .

Mr Sykes: An increase of £21 a year to me and I only get £10 Christmas bonus, I'm £11 worse off.

Mrs Thatcher: Yes, and would you say how much your pension has gone up since November 1978?

Mr Sykes: A percentage of nothing is still nothing.

Mrs Thatcher: I'm sorry, but the facts show that the pension has gone up by sixty-eight per cent and prices have gone up by sixty-one per cent. Those are the facts. On the Christmas bonus, you're right, it is still at £10,

but it's paid for by the taxpayer. We have paid that
£10 . . .

Mr Sykes (interrupting, but inaudible): . . . the cruise
missiles . . .

Mrs Thatcher: . . . through the taxpayers' money each
and every year; whereas Labour didn't. I cannot enter
into a public auction at this election. That public auction
is with money paid through tax and national insurance
contributions of the working population. There are now
some six hundred thousand more pensioners than there
were when we came in.

Mr Sykes: You still call yourself a caring Government?

Mrs Thatcher: I can only care with the money of other
people, I do ask, and the money of other people, I do ask
you, has in fact provided a bigger pension than the rise in
prices.

And I think that during the time of a world-wide
recession to have done that, and to have spent more on
the National Health Service, and more on disabled
people is a very very good record both for Government
and the burden which the twenty-three-and-a-half
million people who are in work, have to bear.

Back in the flat in Downing Street, we discussed the
programme over a drink. The consensus was: much praise
to Mum, and many derogatory remarks about 'Nationwide'.

Ferdy Mount, John Selwyn Gummer, MP for Eye in
Suffolk, David Wolfson, Mum, Dad and I had supper. Then
another speechwriting session got underway to tackle the draft
of the Prime Minister's speech to a rally in Harrogate on
Thursday.

The political vibes seem to be very positive, even if it is still
very early days in the campaign. Stories are coming in on the
grapevine: of young people, first-time voters, turning up at
Conservative branches saying, 'You'd think that I'd be
Labour, but I'm going to vote for you'; of middle-aged voters
who are desperately worried about the Opposition's defence
policy, or lack of it; of council house tenants who slogged to
save up the deposit to buy their house, and recoil at the

thought of having to sell it back under Labour.

1.40 a.m.: The speechwriters having departed, I went into the sitting room to insist that Mum went to bed. This suggestion met with resistance. Mum closed up and locked her completed red boxes, tidied away papers into a briefcase, picked up empty glasses and plumped up flattened cushions – almost anything which delayed having to go to bed. Wide awake, she was far too keyed up to sleep. But I thought that getting her into bed was at least a step in the right direction.

'Goodnight, please try to go to sleep,' I pleaded, feeling rather a bully – albeit, I told myself, a righteous one.

Wednesday, 25 May

When is an address a speech *qua* speech, and when is it just saying a few words off the cuff?

When is a rally really a rally, and how does it differ from a whistlestop, a walkabout, or a three-minute stop?

These were a couple of the questions that Mum threw at Roger Boaden as the train pulled out of Victoria Station for Gatwick. A glance at the day's yellow-bound programme for the Eastern Area, which had her doing 'a whistlestop, address rally, address another rally, a three-minute stop and address a third rally', had momentarily caused waves in the Prime Minister's usually flat calm mind. She wanted to decipher the 'programmese' and to ascertain whether she was required to give an address, a speech or to ad lib at each venue. Moreover, how many people would she be talking to, and for approximately how long?

Roger was displeased. Apparently he had instructed that the term 'rally' shouldn't appear in the day's programme because it had a connotation – of something major necessitating a speech with a script. This, in turn, involves a major exercise with intensive burning-the-midnight-oil sessions with speechwriters in the flat and frantic dawn retypes by Alison and Tessa.

In fact, once we'd translated the jargon the picture became clearer and the distress in the Prime Minister's train compartment evaporated. What the day really entailed was a stint on the hustings in the country, drumming up votes in Norfolk villages and market towns, and at the county showground.

After a flight to RAF Marham, we boarded the campaign bus in particularly high spirits. First, it was a fantastic day weatherwise with blue skies and sunshine that reminded me of Australia. Then, the Labour Party was still tearing itself apart over its 'Keep Polaris/scrap Polaris, as in the Manifesto' split. Last, we were off to see Richard Ryder, the candidate for Mid-Norfolk, and his wife Caroline. They have both worked for Mum and were exceptionally close friends of everyone on the bus. Caroline was on the campaign bus for the 1979 election.

The first village whistlestop was in Narborough, in the South-west Norfolk constituency. Without a loud hailer, but warming to her theme, which would become progressively more spirited throughout the day, Mum told the small crowd: 'I want a very big majority. The Labour Party Manifesto is the most extreme ever and it deserves a very big defeat.'

Back on the bus, and after a ten-minute journey through country lanes, we rolled into the pretty village of Castle Acre, in the North-west Norfolk constituency, for a rally of villagers and Party workers. Some uninvited CND demonstrators had shown up too. The constituency is currently held by Christopher Brocklebank-Fowler – the one Tory to defect to the SDP.

Before Mum got off the bus she was told that one of the brick-bats being hurled at the Tory candidate, twenty-eight-year-old Henry Bellingham, was that he was too young. That gave her her first line. From the back of a horsebox, opposite the village pub' and alongside the fifteenth-century stone Bailey Gate, Mum declared that she had first stood for Parliament when she was twenty-five and that she believed in young people getting in, because it gave them plenty of time to acquire experience.

With thirty years of campaign know-how, and the taunts of hecklers – which are always guaranteed to get her going – Mum didn't do things by halves in Castle Acre. Battling on, with all guns firing, she called for a bumper result from the

country and a bumper result from this constituency. Two
Tornado jets, as if on cue, did a flypast as she spelt out the
Conservative stand on defence: 'Where freedom and justice
are taken away, people know we will go in and get it back.'

She canvassed a tremendous victory and a large majority,
but warned against complacency: 'I do not want you to take
anything for granted. We need every single vote on polling
day.'

We left, running late, about seven minutes after we should
have arrived at the next rally, but the tone for the day had
been set. Nowhere could have turned on a bigger welcome
than the market town of East Dereham. As we arrived, people
leant out of first-floor windows, waved and cheered. In the old
market square, a crowd of about twelve hundred waited for
us. It was an indication of Richard and Caroline Ryder's
terrific local popularity, and a tribute to their hard work in
Mid-Norfolk.

Richard had been Mum's political secretary first in
Opposition and then during her first two years in Number
Ten. Caroline had worked as her secretary when she was
Leader of the Opposition, and had been her Personal
Assistant in Number Ten since 1979. Mum frequently
referred to her as 'my right hand'. She is on leave now, to help
Richard and to have a baby in August.

So pleased were we all to see them both in marvellous form
that I almost missed the bus. I was searching deserted East
Dereham streets for somewhere to buy a bottle with which to
toast them on the bus. Alison and Tessa had better luck in this
direction and emerged from the International Supermarket
with a bottle of sparkling wine. Mum, meanwhile, was telling
Richard's constituents through a loud hailer that her former
political secretary and their candidate was one of the most
warm, kind and conscientious people you could meet, 'so
highly do I think of him as a person'.

She furthered the Conservative cause with all the crusading
zeal appropriate to a position immediately outside a cinema
which was showing a film titled *The Missionary*.

A handful of hecklers made the proceedings interesting, and
they got a dose of the medicine which has made Her Majesty's
Opposition reel in the House of Commons during PM's

Question Time for the past four years. 'What I have given to you are the facts,' she thundered to them in best Iron Lady fashion. 'Yes, there are higher pensions, more doctors and more nurses – a damn sight better than under Labour.'

She might have been coasting up to now, but this wasn't just campaigning, it was combat, and she was relishing every moment of it. 'The National Health Service is safe with us,' she told an enthusiastic crowd which had swelled as she had been speaking.

Richard and Caroline travelled on the bus with us to the next village of Hockering, and on the way we toasted their success with warm sparkling wine out of the bus's plastic cups!

In a brief stop (the three-minute one on the programme), leaning over an open car door, microphone cupped to her mouth, Mum canvassed a small group in the age-old style. No media, just the Prime Minister and locals. One inhabitant welcomed her visit for the excitement of the event. 'This is absolutely fantastic, it's the greatest thing that ever happened to this village, nothing ever happens here,' was her instant verdict on the Maggie show.

A crowd of about three hundred and fifty at Norfolk County Showground heard the Prime Minister give more hecklers a run for their money in a lively performance from a trailer-made platform.

Gordon Reece had dropped in by helicopter, a bit miffed that the authorities wouldn't let him land right on the showground.

Mum concentrated on bashing Labour. Their defence policy was 'a dead loss', she said, their pledge to take Britain out of the Common Market, 'lunacy'. The National Health Service was safe with the Conservatives, who would also deal with unemployment better than Labour. This was too much for a heckler. 'Oh yeah?' he sardonically queried.

'Yes, sir,' barked back Mum with all the clout of the resolute approach, 'Maggie will.' It was her serve now.

'Don't get excited, dear boy, you have a bit more to hear yet, you are going to hear the facts.'

Down on the grass, she spoke to supporters before giving interviews to the local media. The campaign song 'Maggie for

Me' belted out through the speakers. Its jaunty chorus –
words by Ronnie Millar, music by *Hello Dolly*'s composer,
Jerry Herman, and sung by Vince Hill and Lisa Westcott:

> *Who do we want?*
> *Who do we need?*
> *It is a leader who is bound to succeed;*
> *Maggie Thatcher –*
> *Just Maggie for me*

It may not be to everyone's taste, but it was thoroughly in
keeping with Mum's bubbling, boisterous fighting performance at all the day's meetings whatever they'd been – rallies,
whistlestops, walkabouts or three-minute stops.

WEEK TWO

Thursday, 26 May

For the Prime Minister this barely rated as another day, merely a continuation of the previous one. She had been up until past 3.00 a.m., working on her speech for a rally in Harrogate the following evening, because she wasn't happy with it. She had only been in bed an hour or so when the military bands, rehearsing for Trooping the Colour on Horse Guards Parade, right outside her bedroom window, had struck up to cancel finally what remained of her night's sleep.

Downstairs, between 7.00 and 7.30 a.m., Alison and Tessa frantically retyped the previous night's draft of the speech – all sixty-two pages of it. It was going to be one of those days when every available moment was devoted to 'speech-time' – on trains, buses and planes – to get it right before she stood up to deliver it in the Royal Hall in Harrogate at 7.00 p.m.

Our destination that day was Yorkshire, and our schedule was as follows: arrival at Leeds and Bradford Airport at 1.00 p.m.; a fish-and-chips lunch and photocall at Harry Ramsden's Restaurant; two village whistlestops; tours of a dumper truck factory and a police convalescent home; reaching Harrogate at 4.00 p.m., followed by two television interviews. This all adds up to pretty condensed campaigning.

Immediately we had sat down on the Gatwick-bound train Mum, David Wolfson, Michael Spicer and Derek Howe produced copies of the speech and started to slash it down in length. As it was by now an amalgamation of several drafts, the structure and flow had become unbalanced and several points were made more than once.

56

On the plane, they ran through the speech's contents: approach to unemployment; attack on Labour's plan to pull out of the EEC and the jobs that would be put at risk; the Conservative record on social services; home ownership; guarding the peace; and disarmament proposals.

On arrival at Leeds Airport, we transferred to the campaign bus. It was now over to Alison and Tessa to retype the amended speech. The golfball on the typewriter was changed to speech type and Tessa got going. Typing against the clock on a moving bus must, along with playing a trumpet on horseback or cooking on a listing yacht, be one of life's trickier tasks.

They discovered that several gaffes had got into the script during their desperate 7.00 a.m. retype, and on page thirty-eight they had Mum saying: 'Mr Chairman, the greatest thing we can pass onto our children is peach with freedom and justice.' Mum had indignantly altered the 'h' to 'e' with a giant-sized felt-tipped pen.

At Harry Ramsden's Fish and Chip Restaurant in Leeds, which claims to be one of the largest in the world, and where they apparently have no difficulty in serving one and a half million customers a year, we presented a problem.

The episode epitomized disorganization and chaos from almost every point of view: the restaurant's, fellow diner', plus a fair amount of embarrassment to the Prime Ministerial party.

The media mob invaded, seized chairs and surrounded Mrs Thatcher's table, totally enveloping diners who had mistaken-ly chosen the restaurant that day for either a quick or a quiet lunch.

The only person whom I saw make any headway was a determined Yorkshire waitress carrying four pots of tea and booming, 'boiling water coming through', which resulted in a small passage opening up in the otherwise solid wall of humanity.

After consuming a plate of fish and chips for the benefit of the press plus television cameras, Mum spent a few minutes dishing out a portion of fish and chips in the takeaway section of the shop. This was to appease the photographers, who were threatening open revolt at the shambles which were making it practically impossible for them to do their job.

As the Prime Ministerial party made its way back to the bus, Conservative supporters cheered while white-faced CND demonstrators, wearing Klu-Klux-Klan lookalike gear, chanted 'Jobs not Bombs'.

The worst thing about this kind of event is that people who really want to see Mum, and have sometimes waited ages to do so, get pushed and shoved around and trampled on. I, for instance, would like to send another poster of Mum to the pensioner who had her prized one ripped in half by a television crew, because it just happened to be in their view. Prime Ministerial arrivals and departures are becoming as civilized as terraces at football matches.

Down the road, Mum interrupted speech-time to hop off the bus in Menston. This is a suburban village in the Shipley constituency, an area which is basically a dormitory town for Bradford and Leeds.

The boundary changes have been beneficial to the seat, which Marcus Fox, a former Conservative Party Vice-Chairman, has held since 1970. This was a media-less walkabout for Mum, so that she was able to shake hands with almost everyone in the small crowd.

We then proceeded to Otley, a traditionally Liberal town in the Leeds North-west constituency, which stretches from Headingley out to Otley. The candidate here for the Tories is Dr Keith Hampson, who has held the seat since February 1974.

Our destination in Otley was Robert Ogden Holdings, a dumper truck factory. No sooner had we arrived than David Wolfson went off in search of a photocopier to copy the speech, assisted by John Whittingdale.

After serving in a takeaway fish and chip shop only an hour before, Mum's next stunt was to drive a dumper truck fitted with a newly invented electronic device called Albert. This stands for Analogue, Linear, Bi-polar, Electronic Ranging Transducer, and basically stops the truck in the nick of time from colliding with other vehicles or humans by braking automatically when it detects them.

Innately cautious, Mum, in hard helmet, seated in the driver's cab and under close supervision, wasn't about to try out Albert on her bus, the two press buses, or the considerable

crowd which had assembled to watch the Prime Minister at
the wheel. She confined herself to rolling gently backwards for
about six yards, and left it at that.

'No way was I going to go forwards, in case I hit
something,' she said later.

Another ten-minute non-media whistlestop took place
outside Huby village hall, where she was given a warm and
informal welcome by a crowd of old people and a class from a
nearby village school. As three riders and their horses looked
on, and a train sped past, it seemed as though the clock had
been put back and here was an old-fashioned campaign
meeting.

Huby is a village in the sprawling constituency of Skipton
and Ripon, which covers a huge area north of Leeds and
Bradford. It is a new seat, formed out of an amalgamation of
parts of some seven old constituencies. John Watson, the
Member for the old seat of Skipton since 1979, is the Tory
candidate.

Posters were proudly held high: 'Maggie's Fleet for
Downing Street', 'MT and GB' and 'Keep Maggie at the Top,
do what's Best for Britain Vote Tory', they declared in bold
letters.

She shook hands, signed autographs and couldn't have had
a more hearty farewell than the vigorous three cheers which
rang out as she climbed back on the bus.

At the Northern Police Convalescent Home in Harrogate
she spoke to the patients, mostly police officers who were
recovering from injuries they had received in the course of
their duties.

On the bus outside the home she gave two television
interviews. The first was to BBC North, in which she rejected
allegations that she headed an 'uncaring Government'. After
this, straight to the back of the bus, where she asked a female
reporter from Yorkshire Television, 'As one girl to another,
do I need any lipstick?' Yes came the answer, so she
applied some. The camera rolled, more questions, more
answers. A crew from 'Panorama' came on board to film
her during the few minutes' drive to the Majestic Hotel
in Harrogate.

It had been a hectic non-stop three hours for the Prime

Minister, on virtually no sleep and with her major speech still to come.

At the hotel, Alison and Tessa put the speech onto the Autocue tape, with John Whittingdale posted outside the door as henchman to make sure they suffered no interruptions. Mum meanwhile changed and made up, and with a whisky and soda sat down to familiarize herself with the speech, which was now looking good. She said little about the day that she had just spent so hectically, but remarked that it did seem a slow campaign.

After a light supper with David Wolfson, Michael Spicer and Dad she left for Royal Hall, an old theatre which was packed with twelve hundred people. On the stage, under television spotlights, and after the chairman's introduction, she started: 'Mr Chairman, we are approaching the halfway mark in this election. We are going strong. We shall finish strongly. And I believe we shall win. It's a rough campaign. But I never expected our opponents to fight according to Queensbury rules. They seldom do.'

Backstage, Autocue operator, Alex Higgs, sustained by cigarettes and a can of orange drink, concentrated on winding on the tape to follow Mum. Later he remarked how easy a speaker she was to follow.

In other parts of the theatre, journalists filed copy on the telephones and photographers, after something different, poked their lenses through the back of boxes.

The audience watched an attacking performance from Mum:

> Labour's leaders are brave enough in the battle of words. Yet, when it comes to the real battle for economic survival and lasting prosperity, they have no stomach for the fight.
>
> Once again, their Manifesto confirms that in the end Labour always runs away. They are at it again in this election; as fast as their legs will carry them.
>
> They are running away from the need to defend their country.
>
> They are fleeing from the long overdue reform of the trade unions.

They are running out on Europe.

And they are running scared that you might read and understand their Manifesto.

Above all, Labour is running away from the true challenge of unemployment. Its glib promise to create millions of new jobs – or rather, old jobs, or non-jobs – is no more than an evasion of the real problem that has long faced us all.

The Standard, 19 May

"You'll find the party manifestos under fiction, sir."

London Express Service/The Standard

Having, in Cardiff on Monday, attacked the Labour Manifesto's provisions to nationalize savings, she turned her attention to another section of 'The New Hope for Britain':

I thought you might fancy a further instalment. Here is what they say about Europe.

'British withdrawal from the Community is the right

policy for Britain – to be completed well within the lifetime of Parliament.'

Mr Chairman, more than two million British jobs depend on British membership of the Common Market. More than two million. Every single one of those jobs would be at risk.

Then listen to what they say about defence. 'Labour will reduce the proportion of the nation's resources devoted to defence so that the burden we bear will be brought into line with that of the other major European NATO countries.'

To do that would mean cutting Britain's defence by some £4,500 million – equivalent to the entire budget of the Royal Navy.

According to Labour's last defence spokesman, Mr Brynor John, Labour's defence cuts 'would mean a loss of jobs of a minimum of three hundred and twenty-five thousand and probably over half a million'.

Now they claim that they would make sure that their defence cuts didn't lead to unemployment by converting defence factories to making what they call 'useful goods'.

But, even assuming you could make the conversion overnight, who'd buy those goods? Our ex-partners in Europe, who'd just been repudiated by a Labour Britain?

Our American allies, who'd just seen their nuclear bases in Britain closed down by order of a Labour Government – because that's what the Manifesto says – with thousands more British job losses in and around those bases?

Who'd buy from a Labour Britain which had slammed on import controls?

And that's in the Manifesto too.

But far the most chilling sentence for job prospects in this devastating document is this one: 'At the heart of our programme is Labour's new partnership with the trade unions.'

Mr Chairman, it was Labour's old partnership with the trade unions that brought this country to its knees. The strikes, the restrictive practices, the overmanning, the political blackmail – all of it endorsed over and over again by Labour leaders – and not least by the present one.

At the end of the speech, two young bouquet bearers found themselves doing more than just presenting the flowers. Linking arms with Mum, the three of them bowed in unison to the stalls, to the right, to the left, and waved up to the gods.

On the way out Mum turned to see rows of faces to whom she meant leadership and charisma. To show their appreciation they cheered and waved their Union Jacks so hard and fast they became just a blur.

She waited for a few minutes in a cramped upstairs office, the occupant of which, judging by the Che Guevara poster on the wall, might not have been too pleased to see her had he been there.

Mum wished good luck to the candidates, who in turn gave her congratulations and good wishes. The police message then came through that the Prime Ministerial car was ready and that they were anxious to get her away as soon as possible to clear the exit.

Friday, 27 May
Today was a 'high tech' day for the Prime Minister. After her usual morning meetings and press conference at Central Office, we helicoptered down to Reading from Battersea Heliport for our campaign day in the Wessex area.

Ian Gow, who is job-sharing with Michael Spicer the task of accompanying the Prime Minister, is back with us. Michael has gone back to his constituency of Worcestershire South, where he is fortunate enough to enjoy a twenty-two thousand majority.

The day's programme included five visits to micro-electronic, digital, quantized television and computer colour matching factories. In between these tours were sandwiched whistlestops to support candidates: Tony Durant in Reading West; Gerard Vaughan in Reading East; and Michael McNair Wilson in Newbury.

I had decided that this was to be my spell as hack for the day, or, a chance to get a perspective on things from the press·

bus, of which two are following us.

One freelance journalist, Rod Tyler, has dubbed their passengers 'Derek [after press officer, Derek Howe] and the Reptiles'. Whereas Derek and Roger Boaden have christened the campaign package 'Thatcher Tours'.

On board the coaches are ITN and BBC television crews, and photographers and reporters from most of the national dailies and some of the Sundays. Then there is the international press, which Derek irreverently calls the 'foreign funnies'. Today's collection includes representatives from: Asahi Shimbun, Xinhua News Agency (the official Communist Chinese news agency), TV Machete, *Politika, France Soir*, Fuji Telecasting, Suddentschet Rundfunk, *Stern* and *Het Parool*.

This is how a fellow-reptile saw my day in the following morning's *Guardian* [and thanks to the *Guardian* and Julia Langdon for permission to use this piece]:

Mum's the word to keep the hacks at bay
Julia Langdon assumes the role of Carol Thatcher, who is writing a book on the progress of her mother's election campaign.
It was when Mum announced that we were going to spend yesterday looking at the new technology that I decided I'd devote my diary for the day to the doings of the press.

So I packed my tape recorder along with the old technology (my notebook), got someone to lend me a camera (and a photographer from the *Daily Express* to show me how to use it), and joined the rest of the hacks on the press bus in Reading.

I stuck with Mum and Dad for the helicopter down there, and Mum got her hair blown about a bit, which must have been still in her mind when we got to the first factory.

A man was showing her the timer device and suddenly she asked: 'Can I use it to turn on my Carmen rollers?' He looked a bit surprised. She explained that they took fifteen minutes to warm up and it would be awfully useful if they were already hot when she got back to Downing Street in the evening – so he gave her a timer to take home.

I told the hacks I'd try it out. Actually, she already gets other people lined up to turn the rollers on, anyway, but I suppose she wanted to demonstrate her belief in electronics in the homestead.

We go on touring this awfully dull factory, with all the operatives soldering on in the face of the recession. Mum goes around looking awfully grave and interested but Dad looks dreadfully bored and keeps looking at his watch as if he's wondering if it's nearly lunchtime.

I went and interviewed a French journalist from *France Soir*. I asked her a lot of questions about what President Mitterand was up to and what she thought of our politics, and then she asked me who I worked for. She looked astonished when I said I was the Prime Minister's daughter.

Next stop, a shopping centre where Mum made a speech from the back of a lorry all about the Tories being the decisive party with a constructive programme, dogged with determination, etc. I got on top of a bottle bank to see better and then she got back to the high tech' business.

I got it on the tape because my shorthand is a bit rusty. Anyway, if I'm going to write this book I haven't got time to take all the notes. What she said was that she had a sound economic policy which addressed itself to the true cause of unemployment.

'It is only if you do that that you can hope to get the jobs of the future,' she said. She reminded them about how she wanted to put the Great back in Britain. Stimulate new industry, ability to compete, hey presto, we sell goods and that means jobs. 'Ours is the true policy and the one that is likely to produce the best results for our young people.'

More blue rinses, then back in the Robust Bus and moved off so fast that some of the reptiles got left behind. That must have given Dad a good laugh.

He was laughing on the other side of his face at the next place, though. She was enthused by a cellular telephone that you can carry everywhere with you. She was extolling its virtues to the quip 'Ladies and gentlemen of the press' – which isn't what she generally calls them – but when she moved off Dad moved in.

He looked v. worried about this miracle and asked when it would be introduced. The servile young bloke – he'd been calling Mum 'Ma'am' as if she was the Queen – said it would be about 1985. Dad looked very bleak: 'Life is going to be hell,' he said. The guy said it had a Do Not Disturb button, but he didn't seem reassured.

We slipped in a visit to an electronics place and thanked them for winning the Falklands war and then she couldn't miss the chance of making a speech in a village called Thatcham – one of those places where the women wear deerstalkers.

She found the first demo of the day here. A teacher called Dave Curtis shouted 'Shame' and 'Spend it on the schools, then' but the only response he got was from schoolgirls who sniggered and said: 'Ooh look, there's Mr Curtis.'

Ma'am batted on about getting a record majority and promised 'another year of firm, decisive and humane government'.

She sounded as if she was talking about a laboratory experiment. But I wonder what she meant by 'another year'. Perhaps she's going to give up?

At the first stop at Tempatron in Reading – where Mum got her timing device for the hair curlers – I realized that sharp elbows and an ability to stand on tip toe for prolonged periods are helpful if you're ever going to see what's going on.

Even Dad sometimes misses out when Mum gets scooped up by the welcoming managerial committee and he finds himself overtaken by the cantering press corps. On the last election campaign, thanking the managing director after we'd made an eleven-minute tour of his factory, Dad asked if he could come back in quieter times and see what was actually made there. It was carbon paper but he hadn't caught a glimpse of it.

The drill is that photographers and TV crews take up vantage points along the Prime Ministerial route and snap away when she comes into view. One reporter opted out,

Banked-up rows of press photographers focus on Mum as she discusses the merits of snap action bi-metallic thermostats at Tarka Controls in Inverness

The hazards that can be
encountered on the campaign
trail:

Above: CND supporters await
the arrival of the Prime
Minister at Cardiff

Above right: Total immersion on
how bread gets sliced – at the
rate of twenty-eight loaves per
minute. Mum, having donned
white coat and scarf, watches
the slicing and wrapping
machine at Warburton's
bakery in Bolton

Above left: The Opposition in Bristol

Above: 'Thatcher Out' badges being sold by one of Mum's less supportive constituents in Finchley

Right: The hairdo in peril

Left: Hostility on the other side of the street being firmly restrained by Stockport police

– And the politician's assets:

Mum meets one of her younger admirers in Norfolk

These two have the Falkland Islands in common: Mum helps to cut a birthday cake for a Falkland war veteran – 1915 campaign – at Longwell Community Centre near Bristol

As the British are a dog-loving nation, to be photographed with a handsome canine specimen – sporting a Tory sticker – is always a bonus during canvassing

Dad equipped with ear muffs, on board the helicopter (© Roger Boaden)

e campaign consort on the stump: nis in political discussions under the spices of the Conservative candidate, bert Banks, in Harrogate

The Prime Minister's is not a nine to five job. The Prime
Minister works at her red boxes into the small hours of the
morning

On board the campaign bus. *Above:* Too much to do, too little time. An earnest debate in progress, from left, Derek Howe, Michael Spicer, Roger Boaden, Mum and Dad. *Below:* Sharp application of brakes has sent the campaign typewriter flying off the table: Alison and I try to make emergency repairs, watched by Roger Boaden and John Whittingdale. David Wolfson observes from afar

having espied a coffee machine, and was, amidst some of the
most advanced technology in the world, heard to request
assistance on how it worked – an irony which was pointed out
to him several times over by colleagues.

Back on the bus everyone clustered round to hear the
playback of a tape from someone who had actually got close
enough to record some Maggie quotes.

The next stop was a mystery addition. It wasn't on the
press programme and had 'Not to be publicized' beside it in
capitals on the Prime Ministerial one. Either a fashionably
leaked document had blown the secrecy or someone observant
had noticed the giveaway clues to a Maggie visitation – blue
posters and rosettes, crowds with expectant faces, demonstrators and the loudspeaker lorry in position. It was a whistlestop.

In the Honey End Lane shopping precinct in Reading,
Mum extolled the virtues of the local candidates – Tony
Durant in Reading West and Gerard Vaughan in Reading
East – to their party workers and assembled voters.

> I can testify from the Westminster end, of what
> supremely good members you have had, how well they
> serve the interests of their constituencies.
>
> I also come to urge you to vote Conservative for the
> sake of voting Conservative because, first, we are a
> decisive Party with a clear constructive programme,
> knowing exactly where we are going and sticking with
> dogged determination to that way.

Standard stuff, nothing new from the story point of view –
plug candidate, push party – was the consensus from the press
corps. The high-rise fanatics among them had scaled a bottle
bank, which at least afforded an aerial look at the proceedings.

Our next stop was Racal Research in Reading, which is the
world's Number One walkie-talkie manufacturer. The Prime
Minister was allowed a go on the latest model, the Jaguar
Frequency-Hopping Anti-Jamming Radio, of which Oman
has bought £20 million worth.

'Enemy concentration, send in some canvassers', she
hammed it up.

The pluses of the next product she emphasized to the press. It was a cellular radio telephone. 'So much more efficient, news will be quicker', super saleswoman Maggie informed us.

In a speech to unveil a plaque and open the building, she enthused about Racal's success story. Anyone who hadn't read the press hand-out learnt that Racal's annual sales in the last thirteen years had leapt from £15 million to £644 million, and profits from £2 million to £103 million.

It was a performance which, Mum said later, had come to her as she stood up.

'I think that the fact we're going into science-based industries gives countries like ours a new phase in opportunity. We're good at this, not merely good, we're brilliant at fundamental research, we're brilliant at invention', she enthused. She ended her speech with congratulations and a touch of commercialism. 'We hope that by being here today we're advertising you to the rest of the world.'

It was a canteen lunch for her party, while the press were shown out through the fire exit, from where we walked to lunch at the nearby Post House. Some adjourned to the bar, others dived for telephones, and some ate. Hearing Chris Potter of *The Sun* dictating his hot curlers piece, which had become the story of the day, I tried to put him right with my inside knowledge of the Number Ten sequence of switching on the hot rollers, their heating up, setting the Prime Ministerial hair, and so on. This resulted in his having to apologise to the copy-takers on his paper, 'Hang on a moment, I'm being heckled by the Prime Minister's daughter!'

The BBC and several papers, including *The Observer*, *France Soir* and *The Mail on Sunday*, were quite pleased to have caught up. We'd left them behind and they'd had to hitch lifts, divert a Tory transit van and, in the case of the more affluent Dutch, call a cab.

Shortly afterwards, 'She's on the move again' messages went round the room and half-eaten meals were abandoned and glasses drained as we scrambled for the buses.

At another Racal factory, Mum mischievously sabotaged one TV reporter's stand up to the camera. To add authenticity to his claim to be 'on the campaign trail with Mrs Thatcher', he'd organized to have her entourage in the background. But he misjudged the speed with which it was moving towards him. Halfway through his script, the Prime Minister had sneaked up behind him and was peering round him, wide-eyed. The other networks happily filmed this, no doubt as additions to the goof tapes.

Back on the road again, another 'Not to be publicized' whistlestop was made in Thatcham, in between Reading and Newbury. This time the press corps was able to muscle in. Mum made her speech from a loudspeaker van parked beneath a free car park sign. Because of the hecklers and the proximity of Greenham Common, she spelt out the Conservative record on the social services and rammed home the message, 'We are the peace party'.

This was all a bit too much like more of the same for some of the press, and the arrival of the rain definitely made staying on the press bus the preferable option in Thatcham.

Quantel Limited was the fourth factory on the itinerary. On arrival we were handed glossy public relations kits which contained a black and white photo of Mrs Thatcher shaking hands with herself on a television screen to demonstrate the skills of Quantel's new electronic Paintbox – a kind of television graphics gadget.

The stills photographers decided that Mum and the Paintbox was the picture they wanted, and volunteered not to cause any bother if they could get set up as soon as possible. First, the lighting posed a problem: house lights on; house lights off; some on; some off. A television spotlight was produced, shone at about eight different angles, daylight filter put on, and bounced off the ceiling before some lighting formula was agreed upon by everyone.

The who stood where and how far away had to be sorted out. 'Come on chaps, you've got plenty of room, you can do it,' one stills photographer informed a TV crew. Another saw a potential obstruction: 'If the Leather Jacket comes in front, he gets the treatment.' Leather Jacket – who later transpired to be from the German magazine, *Stern* – stayed put.

'Come on, half a pace back, be sports,' pleaded the *Daily Express*. 'I don't want to go back, I don't actually think you need to be any further back, frankly, I think we're back far enough,' overruled the *Daily Mail*.

Mum eventually arrived, but if the photographers thought she was there for their benefit, she had other ideas. Sitting down rather eagerly, she was looking forward to her electronic painting lesson from artist, Martin Holbrook, who found that he had a quick and keen learner on his hands.

'It's so easy to use because all the time you're just drawing,' he demonstrated.

A photo of Mum came up on the screen. 'I think you could have found a more flattering one,' she protested.

'We had such short notice, you know, blame the newsmen not me,' defended Martin. Newsmen present bristled.

'I can do frightful things with this, I can turn you round very easily. Using this little joystick here, I can reduce you in size,' carried on Martin, putting the Paintbox through its paces.

'You couldn't do a different hairstyle, so I could have a look?' queried Mum. Martin continued onto the machine's myriad fixing, fudging and fogging capabilities.

'If we want to have you shaking hands with somebody – this is an excellent example of forgery.' That word rang alarm bells with Mum, who was a barrister for six years before she went into Parliament.

'So you could never never use pictures again in court as evidence after this, because it would have absolutely no veracity at all,' she twigged. 'You could prove that I was with someone I'd never seen.'

Martin realized that Mum's fidgeting fingers were longing to have a go on the Paintbox and, being politically tactful, he invited her: 'If you'll ignore the fact that it's a red line I'm asking you to use there, I'd love you to sign your name.'

This proved as fraught with problems as getting her to write 'Dear Elector' and 'Yours sincerely, Margaret Thatcher' on her election address had proved at the printers in Finchley on the previous Saturday.

Dissatisfied with her first attempt, she demanded 'Can you wipe that off and I'll start again.' More problems. 'It's a lousy machine,' she accused.

'Come on, stencil that off, now look that's terrible, take it off.' The usually authoritative 'Margaret' was looking a touch dyslexic on the screen.

'Oh Lord, it's simply dreadful, you can't sign your name on this thing. Where am I?'

Martin offered expert help, 'No, I want the cross,' insisted Mum, determined that however erratic her name might look, the 't' at the end of Margaret was going to be crossed.

'Let me show you something sinister,' Martin volunteered and, as Mum saw her shrinking signature heading for a blank cheque, she joked, 'It'll bounce'.

Put up 'Vote Conservative' someone suggested. 'No, "Vote Thatcher", it's shorter,' countered Mum, who then changed her mind. 'Put up "Vote Conservative", that means there's 650 seats.'

'This is where I have to start spelling, I only draw pictures, my job's on the line at this point,' a worried Martin thought out loud.

Up came 'Vote Conservative'. 'It would be much quicker to design our election address,' said Mum, the attraction of the machine growing on her.

'We're going to be here till midnight,' realized Mum. Whereupon the photographers, who had no intention of doing that, and who had had their patience stretched by her electronic doodles, took this as their cue to remind her of their existence.

Bill Rowntree of the *Daily Mirror* took charge of the proceedings. 'Mrs Thatcher, you've probably gathered the stills photographers have been waiting for this photograph all afternoon. If you could go round by the set, so we have this multiple image of you, it would make a marvellous picture for us, please.'

Playtime over, posing time began. Another TV made it five Maggies, the original and two pairs shaking hands with each other. Massed clicking and motorized whirls of film winding on meant satisfaction all round. But, unbelievably, the next day not one of the pictures appeared in any newspaper.

While we had been inside, absorbing the high tech' world of quantized television, our campaign bus, which was parked outside, had been at the centre of a bomb scare drama.

On board were John Whittingdale, Tessa Gaisman and driver, Ron Sharp. John, sitting on the back seat heard ticking. Ron came back to have a listen, and also heard the panic-provoking, regular tick-tick-tick. Ultra security-conscious because of headlines in the papers about an IRA hit squad, thought to be on the move in London, they called in the plain-clothes policemen from a nearby car.

They confirmed the ominous ticking, coming apparently from under the back seat, and swung into action to organize explosive sniffer dogs to come to investigate.

Vital moments passed horribly slowly until it was suggested to Ron, 'See what happens if you turn the engine off?'

Ignition switched off, simultaneously the ticking stopped.

Its source: the bus's rear right-hand indicator. The sniffer dogs were halted in their tracks and there were several red faces on the bus . . ..

We dropped into Instrumental Colour Systems in Newbury, where Mum soldered the final link in a microprocessor board and was delighted when the tester pronounced it up to standard.

Finally, at Newbury Race Course, she gave an impromptu press conference in the bus before we left by helicopter for Battersea. She noted that the most universal issue of the campaign tended to be the economy, but that this time defence was running almost abreast. 'I think that there is much more worry, a greater feeling about the importance of defence than I've ever encountered in previous elections,' she said.

She finally snuffed out the issue which Foreign Secretary Francis Pym had raised last week, on which she disagreed with him and about which she had been questioned all week – that of the dangers of too large a Tory majority and too small an Opposition. 'We were a small party in Opposition after 1945, we were very effective,' she stressed.

Looking ahead to the following week, she was asked whether she thought there was any possibility of a pick-up in the Alliance vote, in view of the appalling state of the Labour Party:

> It's very difficult to foretell what happens in the last fortnight of an election campaign, because you have got the 'don't knows' making up their minds progressively.
> The Alliance isn't really a Party, it hasn't got any basic

unifying principles on which to go forward. Note, Point Number One, those who left the Labour Party did not go and join the Liberal Party, which is itself very varied because there've always been two groups of Liberals, the old-fashioned Liberal and the person who's almost indistinguishable from Labour; so you've got that great spectrum.

Those who left the Labour Party didn't even join the Liberal Party, they formed something separate and within that separate SDP you've got a spectrum of views.

Really, you have not got a cohesion at all, you've got a miscellany.

Asked if she was now more than cautiously optimistic about the result, she replied confidently but humbly: 'I am cautiously optimistic.'

Back at Number Ten Downing Street, she met Conservative Party Chairman Cecil Parkingson, Ian Gow, David Wolfson and Ferdinand Mount. According to them, the vibes were that it would be odd if the Alliance, after the Steel summit at Ettrick Bridge, and given the state of Labour, didn't show some increase in the polls next week.

The polls at present are in agreement about some strengthening of the Conservative lead. The MORI poll for the *Daily Express* shows the highest lead so far in the campaign – 22 per cent. Marplan and Harris in the last two days have both shown leads of 15 per cent.

As she packed to go to the Williamsburg Summit in the United States, Mum said that the campaign would get dirty next week, that the crucial period was still to come.

She loathes personalized dirty tricks' attacks, because she feels strongly that elections should be fought on issues of policy not mud slinging against individuals.

She'd been irritated, too, by those who had posed the problems of a landslide majority. As a professional campaigner, she didn't believe that there is such a thing as winning too well. Not once since the start of this campaign have I heard her hint that she thought it was all in the bag, or would be a walkover – no matter what the commentators said, or the polls predicted. She has fought to win and win with as big a majority as possible. She hasn't suffered from the Number Ten hang-up which has afflicted some previous Prime Ministers – a difficulty in or distaste for getting back on the hustings after a spell in office. She has simply got on with it, campaigning as hard as she did in Opposition at the last election.

Dad, wisely, took the Bank Holiday weekend seriously and headed off to our flat at Scotney Castle in Kent – which also doubles as his golfing pad – to get in a few rounds of golf and to take a break from his part as campaign consort.

Mark was already in America and wouldn't be back for at least another week, so that I spent the weekend in a virtually deserted Number Ten trying to catch up with this diary.

The combination of a Bank Holiday weekend and Mum's absence in the United States at Williamsburg provided a very welcome intermission from the election trail for everyone who, last week, had slogged around on the planes and buses of 'Thatcher Tours' to Bristol and Cardiff, Dover and Deal, Norfolk, Yorkshire and Reading.

Mum's weekend, however, contained absolutely no recreational prospects. She packed on Saturday morning and had her hair done before leaving to fly across the Atlantic to President Reagan's seven-nation summit in Williamsburg, Virginia. The other leaders there were: President Mitterand of France; Chancellor Kohl of West Germany; Prime Minister Fanfani of Italy; Pierre Trudeau, Prime Minister of Canada; and Yasuhiro Nakasone, Prime Minister of Japan.

Such summit outings have a public image of being a bit of a junket. Having been on several myself – Mum's visits to President Carter and President Reagan, a whirlwind tour of India, Saudi Arabia, the Gulf States and Oman, and a visit, when she was Leader of the Opposition, to China, Japan and Hong Kong – I can testify that they are precisely the opposite.

Television coverage may show the principal against a back-drop of tropical palm trees, visiting some exotic landmark, or tucking into a gargantuan banquet in sumptuous surroundings, but usually the schedule is a series of one-night stops which make shuttle diplomacy look quite leisurely in comparison.

In Williamsburg, because of the time difference, Mum would have to open the after-dinner discussions at about 2.00 a.m. her time. The following day consisted of church, more meetings, a press conference, and then it was just time to catch the overnight flight back to London.

She arrived back on Monday with the summit backing Britain's road to recovery. The six other nations had agreed optimistically that recovery is on the way, that economic policies like Britain's are the best way to bolster and sustain it, that Polaris and the French nuclear deterrent should not be put into arms control talks with the Russians, and that there is no instant cure for unemployment. 'A quick cure is a quack cure', Mum declared at her press conference.

Meanwhile, on this side of the Atlantic, her principal opponents, the Labour Party and the Alliance, had been indulging in some summiteering of their own. These emergency meetings had resulted in both leaders – Michael Foot and Roy Jenkins – remaining at the head of their respective parties, but with somewhat phantom roles to play. They were to take a back seat in favour of men who were thought to be more electorally popular: Labour Deputy, Denis Healey; and Liberal Leader, David Steel, respectively. Chris Potter of The Sun *described Denis Healey's new prominence in the Labour Party's campaign as 'the unleashing of the beast'. But, would he turn out to be a paper tiger?*

The Alliance had spent two and a half hours meeting on Sunday at David Steel's home in the Scottish border village of Ettrick Bridge. This had been dubbed by some as the Shirley Williamsburg Summit. The

The Sun, 1 June

London Express Service/The Sun

Alliance's twelve-member campaign committee had decided that David Steel should move both centre stage and centre screen, being a particularly televisual personality, and take on the major television appearances. David Steel reacted tactfully to the changes: 'What we recognize is the criticism that I have not been perhaps as prominent in the campaign as I should have been.'

He would be de facto *leader in between now and 9 June. An actual change in leadership, the meeting had concluded, would be counterproductive, especially as the Alliance was trying to promote its image of unity.*

The Sun, 31 May

"I ASSURE YOU THAT ROY IS STILL PLAYING A VITAL ROLE IN OUR CAMPAIGN!"
London Express Service/The Sun

Michael Foot, on a similar Independent Radio phone-in to the one that Mum had attended the previous Sunday, also spoke out against swapping leaders mid-campaign. This time, he was dealing with his own leadership. He told Peter Allen that he 'would not dream of resigning as leader at this stage'.

'I have never run away from anything in my life, I would not run away from this one,' he said.

Both Michael Foot and Roy Jenkins are being blamed, in what has become very much a personality campaign – Maggiefesto, one mini cartoon dubbed the Conservative Party's Manifesto – for their parties' poor showing in the opinion polls.

The Government's lead, which everyone expected to decrease once serious campaigning got under way, has in fact consolidated and strengthened.

I remembered my mother at Chequers, the weekend after the election announcement, warning me in a pep talk – I have a reputation for jittery nerves during campaigns – that from then on media coverage would be along the lines of Tory lead falters/shrinks/halves, and so on.

Michael Foot is regarded by his party as an electoral liability with few voters managing to visualize him as Prime Minister, and therefore the Labour Party as the alternative government. Roy Jenkins is thought to be the culprit because he has not been the dynamic catalyst to push the SDP bandwagon along. Hence, both are being relegated to second billing.

The Alliance's failure to make an impression on the electorate is even more surprising considering the down-and-out state of the Labour Party, which commentators are describing in phrases like 'the day the Labour Party fell apart', and practically writing if off as a serious contender in this election race.

Not who will win on 9 June, but the size of the Conservative majority and who will come second seem to be the most talked-about points in this campaign at present. But then things can change overnight.

The next week looks like being a hold-your-breath week. When will the Alliance bandwagon start to roll? How fast? How many percentage points will they move up in the polls? Will they take more seats from Labour, or from the Conservatives? How many people are offput by the ongoing predictions of a Tory landslide, and are therefore tempted to vote tactically – for the SDP – and thereby let a Labour Government in by default?

Tuesday, 31 May

The Prime Minister, back on the stump – this time up in Scotland – wasted no time in drawing her audience's attention to the parlous predicament of the Opposition parties. She was addressing a rally of over a thousand in, appropriately enough, David Steel's old school, George Watson's College, Edinburgh.

> Mr Chairman, you may have noticed that I've been away. It was only for two days. And I must say, now that I'm back, that nothing much seems to have changed.
>
> The Labour Party, the Liberals and the SDP all had meetings last weekend to decide whether to change their policies, or their leaders, or both. All are still refusing to face real issues.
>
> We, on the other hand, are sticking with our policies, and, I understand, our leader.

Behind me on the platform sat the Conservative candidates. In front were George Younger, Secretary of State for Scotland, and Dad. The school assembly hall had been rapidly converted from its usual use by the addition of sellotaped posters of Mum, in between and below the formal gilt-framed portraits of former principals.

Presumably to emphasize the point that the SDP is only the recycled Labour Party, Mum tarred both of them with the same brush: 'The last Labour government, in which Mr Healey was Chancellor and the SDP leaders were prominent members, and which latterly was kept in office by the Liberals – that was the Government which had to be rescued by the international community from the folly of the very policies which Labour would now like to try again.'

Later in her speech, she dealt with the Labour Party smears that she intended to dismantle the National Health Service. She employed the same method that she used against hecklers – the facts.

'And I want to knock on the head, once and for all, the scares that the Labour Party are putting around about pensions and the National Health Service.

'You may remember, they tried the same tactic during the 1979 election. It didn't work then, and it won't work now.'

Applause burst from the audience; this was one of fifty-one clap lines, the speech equivalent of a joke's punchline, scattered throughout this hour long – too long – speech. Its length was partly due to the fact that Mum couldn't read the

Autocue because the television lights up in the gallery were blinding her. So, she ad-libbed some parts and went back to her script for others, not an ideal way of making a speech.

She once likened the process of composing a speech to giving birth – painful. She puts considerable effort into her speeches and never ever comes cold to someone else's script, merely reading it out. This makes speech-writing rather a laborious process at Number Ten, and explains why every evening in this diary reads 'More speech-writing'.

During this election, Ferdy Mount has done almost all of the drafts. They are then discussed and revamped by whoever happens to be around – David Wolfson, Ian Gow, Michael Spicer – usually into the early hours of the morning. Themes are changed, contents altered – what you say, how you say it – speeches which read well don't necessarily speak well. Then there is the problem of a bad hall (modern ones with low ceilings) or an unresponsive audience, which might sabotage the success of the oration.

Dad plays a self-appointed, unofficial part in solving this last problem. Rather less obtrusively than the fellow who, during those recorded audience-participation television shows, pops out with a card on which is written 'applause' or 'clap now', he is always first off the mark to lead the clapping or to drum up support with hearty and bass-toned 'Hear hear's'.

In Harrogate, he had notched up nineteen 'hear hear's' and wasn't on bad form in Edinburgh either.

The speech panic for the evening's address had begun on the plane, which had travelled up from London at lunchtime. David Wolfson, Michael Spicer and Mum had simultaneously fastened their seat belts, snapped open briefcases and fished out copies of the speech. As we taxied out to take off, they started axing sentences and sections.

Throughout the flight to Edinburgh – to the consternation of Tessa and Alison a few rows back, to whom all this new stuff meant endless last minute desperate retypes – Mum carried on scribbling amendments in the margin.

As the undercarriage touched the tarmac on the runway, the speech still hadn't got an ending which Mum considered suitably rousing. In a suite at the Caledonian Hotel, she sat down to familiarize herself with the speech, and to work out the last lines. Meanwhile Alison and Tessa, at supersonic speeds, bashed out the final few pages and the Autocue tape. Twenty minutes before she was due to leave, I popped my head round the door and asked, 'Anything I can do?'

'I just want the last three pages of my speech,' she said. On cue, David Wolfson came flying in, having obviously just ripped the pages out of the typewriter as the key added the full stop.

Mum added an extra line in felt-tipped pen. 'And let no one think it will be easy. The only poll that counts is the count on Polling Day. So let us go forth strong in will, tireless in action, confident that our cause will triumph.'

On arrival at George Watson's College, we waited for a few moments, chatting to George Younger and the candidates in a room off the hall.

Mum hopped up when she spotted a roll of blue 'Maggie In' stickers lying on a table, tore one off and slapped it on the lapel of my Marks & Sparks (ex-hers) jacket.

A precedent had been set for speech dramas in Edinburgh during the 1979 election campaign. I only returned from Australia for the last ten days, so I missed it, but Roger Boaden and others who had been there had the episode clearly etched on their memories.

Mum, preparing to address a rally at Leith Town Hall, was in a last-minute frazzle about her speech. Five minutes after she should have left the hotel, having only just taken the curlers out of her hair, she was found with scissors and paste in hand cutting and glueing sections of the speech together on the floor in an against-the-clock rehash. Arrows and unintelligible notes pointed the way to the next sentence, as the script began to look like a collage.

The net result was that several of the pages got stuck together as the light on the lectern dried out the glue. This not only shortened the performance but also did not exactly add to smooth continuity.

At least things hadn't been so bad this evening. As we left the hall, a handful of demonstrators voiced their protests. One kicked quite hard the passenger door of the car in which I was travelling, which didn't worry me, except that I think that anyone who takes a swing at an accelerating vehicle needs their brains testing. Off balance for a second, and they might fall under the wheels of the next car in the convoy, or get their foot caught in the mudguard, very possibly losing a limb.

From Edinburgh, we flew up to Inverness for the only overnight stop of the campaign tour. Mum was relaxed and relieved that her major speech was over. Shortly before we landed, Mum was told that there would be bagpipes to welcome her and laughingly she asked the air hostesses for a couple of miniature bottles of whisky to present to the pipers.

There was quite a crowd of supporters to meet her, but I missed most of the reception because of a rather shaking and tragic incident. As we left the building, Jimmy Anderson, a well-known local freelance photographer, collapsed on the kerb. One of Mum's security men and several others carried him inside and attempted to revive him, without apparent success.

Later, at the hotel, we learned with sadness that he had died of a heart attack. His son was due to be married on Saturday, so Mum sat down and wrote a note to his widow.

There wasn't much work Mum could get on with, so she took the opportunity of getting to bed relatively early. Before she went she was delighted to hear from Alison that the Number Ten switchboard had received loads of calls praising her performance on 'Panorama', which had been taped that morning in Number Twelve Downing Street, the Government's Chief Whip's Office.

She is still anxious to know how she comes over in interviews and, although much less nervous than she used to be, she is not at ease. I still don't think that her animation and her magnetic personality always come over terribly effectively on the television.

While she was having her hair and make-up done before 'Panorama', she was a bit apprehensive because so much hinges on these few major end-of-campaign media interviews. Each one is an opportunity to make it or muff it. Her only worry afterwards was that she had called Sir Robin Day Mr Day throughout. No matter now, the vibes were that it had been a positive performance.

Downstairs Alison, Tessa and I had a drink with David

Boddy – a laid-back New Zealander who, until he left to launch the successful new magazine, *Out of Town*, had been director of press at Conservative Central Office. He had organized the press buses in 1979 and returned now to help out doing just that for the final week. Hopefully, he will reduce the rugger-scrum nature of walkabouts, which is irritating to Mum and infuriating for the press. At this very moment several members of the press corps are washing down what had apparently been a fairly ordinary Chinese meal with a few nightcaps . . . .

Wednesday, 1 June

This was the day that things started to hot up. By this, I mean the pressure and tempo of the campaign rather than the weather, which, this morning, turned on un-June-like, bleak, chilly, grey skies in Inverness.

The pace of the campaign has moved up from relatively low-key, pre-Williamsburg into a high gear, heralding the start of a build-up to the finishing straight.

It is always hard to keep the momentum of an election campaign going for even three weeks, not to let it lag, or to get forced onto the defensive or to peak too early.

Today is our first full day back on the road after the Bank Holiday weekend and Williamsburg, so there is a certain amount of cranking up to be done.

Our Scottish morning consisted of two visits of three-quarters of an hour apiece to a thermostat factory in Inverness and a cashmere and woollen factory in Elgin. After a lunch-time flight South, we were to drop in on a bakery and a brewery in the Manchester area. Add to that nine media interviews, plus the hassles and logistics of getting around, and it wasn't hard to see that it would be a demanding and exacting day for the Prime Minister.

She started the day in very good spirits, having made the most of what was likely to be her last even half decent night's sleep until after it's all over.

8.00 a.m.: In her suite in the Station Hotel, Inverness, John Whittingdale briefed the Prime Minister for local interviews

on the overnight news, on the analysis of the latest polls –
which are being interpreted to show that the Alliance is
moving upwards – on what the papers are saying, and on
Scottish facts and figures.

The first interview was to be with Grampian Television,
and they had already set up downstairs in Robbie's bar. Mum
said goodbye to hotel staff on the way down, and I followed
with Dad, who always likes to sit in on television interviews.
'How long is the transmission, when will it go to air, how
much of me is in shot?' she asked the interviewer as the studio
man set the voice levels. This was followed by one false start,
which is unlike her, when she muffed an answer and asked to
start again.

The interview went well, with questions about em-
ployment, Conservative electoral prospects in Scotland
– where Labour holds twice as many seats – and the
railways.

When it was finished, she turned to me to ask how much
time we had before departure. 'Five minutes,' I said after
consulting my programme.

'Well,' she declared, jumping up, 'I don't think we should
sit in the *bar*,' which displayed her innate distaste for such
surroundings at 8.45 a.m. and an instinct for the fact that
being spotted in there could dent the image!

We left the Station Hotel in a convoy of cars. It had proved
impossible to get the campaign bus up to Inverness and down
South again in time for the rest of the itinerary.

9.00 a.m.: We arrived at Tarka Controls which, the briefing
told us, 'was established with the assistance of the Highlands
and Islands Development Board in the autumn of 1971 to
manufacture Snap Action Bi-Metallic Thermostats and Safety
Cut Outs for the Domestic Appliance Market'.

After Albert (the device which stops dumper trucks before
they actually hit the human or vehicle towards which they are
heading), which we had seen demonstrated in Yorkshire on
Thursday, and five micro-electronic factories in Reading on
Friday, I began to suspect that someone responsible for
drawing up the programme had a fetish about gadgets.

In cracking form, Mum whipped around the shop floor.

This excerpt from the official tour programme indicates that there was nothing *ad hoc* about the VIP route:

> Enter Production Area – go to alley between Z3 and Z4 Sections
> Meet – John and Tom
> Murial and Winnie +
> Z3 Assembly team and Z4 coverers.
> Walk towards Moulding Section and stop just past Arkburg Automatic Moulding Machines.
> Meet – Magaret and Betty
> Rae and Ben
> Moulders in Vicinity (Heather)
> Split Shift Girls.

Thanks to the calming balm and organization of David Boddy, who'd staked the place out beforehand to ascertain. vantage points for photographers and directed them accordingly, the ghastly media crush which had characterized all previous such visits was avoided.

Photographers and TV crews were one step ahead of their quarry, albeit often banked up to quite an altitude, looking through their lenses to record the Prime Minister looking at some aspect of production.

The camel-coloured suit – as opposed to Tory-blue clothes – that Mum was wearing wasn't an accident of choice. She had had the suit made from cloth which Johnstons of Elgin had presented to her on a previous occasion, and she wanted to wear it to show them.

On arrival at Elgin she complained that we'd passed several supporters and school children who'd waved, and with whom she would have liked to have talked – but time was too tight.

She didn't waste any of that commodity touring the factory, or maybe the speed which had about a hundred of us, her party and press, jogging behind to keep up had something to do with the fact she'd seen it all before. We played a kind of hide-and-seek in and out of mile-long lengths of cashmere tartan, on their way to becoming scarves, stoles and rugs.

In the factory shop, Mum was presented with a very fetching tam o'shanter and matching scarf. She instantly modelled the scarf for photographers but refused to put on the tam o'shanter. 'Too gimmicky,' she excused herself, which I interpreted as Maggie-ese for 'I don't want my hair squashed before the telly interviews'.

My twin brother, Mark's, antics in the Sahara Desert last year, when he went missing during a motor rally, had influenced the wording on one banner which I spotted in the crowd as we left the factory. It read: 'Thatcher, get lost in the desert'.

We then travelled by car to RAF Lossiemouth, passing on the way the birthplace of a previous inhabitant of Number Ten, Ramsay MacDonald. If we have difficulty with the Downing Street domestic arrangements, so did he. When he moved in, he was obliged to furnish the house with furniture and linen from the Co-Op sales, while his family always ate breakfast in the State Dining Room because the Board of Works paid for the coal to heat it.

On the flight to Manchester, the colossal workload that Mum was facing over the next few days dawned on her. She looked through the horrendous itinerary to insert speech-time for each epic address. Suddenly it seemed that too much had been left to her with no one to help.

I reflected ironically that in American presidential campaign cover stories in *Time* magazine one reads about the activities of advisers, aides and flunkies, all beavering away. We are lamentably short of them. The fact that so far the campaign has gone immensely well for Mum and the Conservatives disguises this void. Fast-moving bandwagons skim bumps rather than hit them, but the whole campaign seems to have its hit-and-miss moments on the back-up side of things. The fact that all the indicators are that Mum will win and that she looks a winner, in no way lessens the effort for her, nor the strenuous workload she will have to bear over the next eight days. In addition, several major television appearances have been crammed into the schedule – 'TV Eye' tomorrow night, 'Weekend World' on Sunday, and two more on Monday and Tuesday. This all combines to make us a touch uptight.

At Manchester Airport she toured the new extension, which took the form of a fast-moving, crushed and crushing walkabout. One small boy, enjoying a ride in an aeroplane machine, was overcome with shyness when a Prime Ministerial 'hello' and swivelling TV cameras and clicking lenses interrupted his joyride.

Mum was momentarily non-plussed, too, when her advance was checked by the obstacle of welded-to-the-floor cafeteria-type seating and tables. They spelt dead-end, climb-over, or go-round. Mum left it to her security man to navigate an exit from this Formica-topped table maze.

It was then on to a brief glimpse of the 'gastronette' – the gourmet end of the new eatery – and a spin around the duty-free. The police didn't seem to relish the approach of the Maggie show in full flight. One remarked to his mate, 'Let them go, there are more troops over the other side,' and radioed a warning ahead.

I dived in and out of the throng, taking flowers that Mum had been given to save their petals from total destruction and to leave her with both her hands free.

She, if she saw anything of the new airport development, must have found it almost as novel an experience as supermarket shopping in Finchley on the first Saturday of the campaign. As a travelling Prime Minister, check-ins, duty-free shops and self-service restaurants are not part of the routine. Usually her car drops her off at the bottom of the aircraft steps or, if she is running ahead of time, she might kill a few minutes in the VIP lounge.

The new VIP lounge was our next stop. On this occasion it doubled as a TV studio, and Mum gave an interview to Granada TV.

At Warburtons, a much-respected old family bakers in Bolton, we got togged up in white coats and head gear – there was a choice. Mum went for a white headscarf, I chose a trilby, while others opted for cardboard versions of those tissue-paper hats which drop out of Christmas crackers.

I learnt a lot about Warburtons: it produces a million loaves a week; and the slicing and wrapping machine copes with twenty-eight loaves a minute. All this was thanks to a personalized tour from co-chairman, Tom Warburton.

As advance guard, we skated around ahead of Mum and her accompanying razza-matazz. A bakery photograph of the

Prime Minister inspired one newspaper caption writer. *The Guardian* ran the picture with the question, 'The most successful thing since sliced bread?'

Outside, Mum had a part to play in one entrant's bid to win a trip to Amsterdam – the prize in the National Tea Making fortnight for Cub Scouts. The basic idea was that the cubs had to make tea for as many people as possible during a given period and in particular for a special period.

Operating on the Nothing Ventured, Nothing Gained principle, Peter Gregory of Bolton had, back in May, written to the Prime Minister to ask her: 'Is there any chance that you will be in or near Bolton during the two weeks, because our newspaper says you may be, but it will be a secret until the day before. We would love to make you a nice cup of tea, because we know your throat will be very dry from making speeches to get people to vote for you.'

He was spot on, the cuppa was very welcome and the Prime Minister declared that Peter Gregory made a delicious cup of tea. In her, Peter also found a co-recruiter of special people. Mum summoned ITN's Michael Brunson out from behind his camera to take a sip and sign the card.

'Where's Max Hastings?' she enquired. But it transpired that the first man into Port Stanley was taking a nap elsewhere in order, as he explained later to Mum, to stay awake to inverview her on the flight back to London.

The rowdiest demonstration of the tour greeted us outside a Stockport brewery. Furious demonstrators brandished banners and shouted slogans.

Security got Mum inside, but I had to lock the doors of my car and sit there to the taunts of 'Tory Scum' until we could move on and drive into a car park at the rear.

Via a labyrinth of corridors, I caught up with the official party which was peering into mash tuns, an early stage of the brewing procedure. From there we proceeded to look at the coppers with the aroma of hops, and then on to the fermentation process and the heavy odour of yeast. Mum, usually a non-beer drinker, surveyed a-hundred-and-fifty barrel tanks filled with the stuff.

The rest of the party left in the campaign coach, while Mum and Dad exited by car, which is more manoeuvrable in a security situation. Later on, like a tug approaching a liner, we took the Prime Minister and Denis on board. There was never a chance, though, that Mum could relax during the ten-minute drive to the airport. A BBC film crew had booked her for two interviews. Nick Witchell, in his, zeroed in on the SDP threat:

> **Nick Witchell:** Mrs Thatcher, one full week to Polling Day to go, do you feel at all threatened by this apparent surge of support for the Alliance?
> **Margaret Thatcher:** Whatever the polls say, and they'll go up and down as I warned at the beginning, we carry on in exactly the same way. We laid out our Manifesto, we campaigned vigorously, and we work hard right until the polling stations close, so we don't take a great deal of notice of the polls, we just work.
> **Nick Witchell:** But, do you feel that your position could be threatened by a surge of support for the Alliance?
> **Margaret Thatcher:** If there were a surge of support for the Alliance, they're working harder to take our seats than Labour seats, and if you look at the result of the by-elections, they've taken more of our seats than Labour. So the threat is that if they get more votes, they in fact would put in a Labour Government, and I doubt very much whether that would be the wish of people who are voting for them.

At the airport, Mum spent the minutes waiting for everyone else to get on the plane talking to the prospective Tory candidates. Peter Ridgway, Manchester Blackley; Dave Eager, Manchester Central; John Kershaw, Manchester Gordon; Fred Silvester, Manchester Withington; and Joan Jacobs, Manchester Wythenshawe.

The official photographer had gone missing, so Roger Boaden deputized for the formal shot at the back of the bus.

On board, Mum gave an interview to Max Hastings (now woken up). Although her immediate reaction to giving yet another interview is often 'Oh no', once she gets going she is like a car starting up from stationary, going through the gears to overdrive in record time, and staying there.

1 June

A question mildly sympathetic to the SDP didn't get a sleepy reply, however exhausted the interviewee may have been: 'The SDP MPs should have stayed within the Labour Party and fought from within it. But they hadn't got the guts.'

In fact, she thinks the same about anyone who bails out and takes the easier option, including candidates who desert a marginal seat at the offer of a safe one.

Back at Number Ten she looked exhausted, but added, 'I am not allowed to be'. Speech-writing lay ahead with barely a moment's intermission. The speech for the next day's rally in Birmingham required attention.

Later, the news of Deputy Labour Leader, Denis Healey's, Falklands outburst in Selly Oak, Birmingham, came through. There, he'd said: 'She is wrapping herself in a Union Jack and exploiting the services of our soldiers, sailors and airmen and hoping to get away with it.'

The accusation of glorying in slaughter deeply horrified her but, as she knew she would have the opportunity to deal with it at the following day's press conference, phone calls were made to Cecil Parkinson and the decision taken that he should provide the initial response.

If within Number Ten it was all politics behind closed doors, outside it was pageantry under the floodlights. A performance of Beating Retreat by mounted bands, trumpeters, massed bands, pipes and drums of the Household Division was in progress.

'Do look out at the Household Cavalry,' Mum yelled down to me, papers in hand, barefoot on the landing, straight out of a meeting in the sitting room.

From my room I had the perfect view. Horse Guards Parade looked like a film set, or something out of a fairy tale. Against the romantic backdrop of Whitehall, lit by giant white meteor-bright floodlights, the bands' brass instruments glinted, horses' tails swished and the plumb-line-straight snowy plumes on the cavalry helmets lifted slightly in the evening breeze.

A buglar sounded Handel's *Retreat*, followed by the *Hallelujah Chorus*, *Nightfall in Camp* and the National Anthem before the dramatic *March Off*.

The modern ceremony of Beating Retreat denotes the end

of the working day. On Horse Guards Parade, the floodlights were out, the Household Cavalry and the Guards had long since departed, but in Number Ten the lights still burned bright.

Mum kicked off her shoes and tucked her feet underneath her at one end of the sofa. Beside her, on a side table, the clock showed the late hour. Above it hung a painting of Chequers. In front of her stood the coffee table, decorated with a map worked in wood of the Falkland Islands, made by the apprentices at the Royal Aircraft Establishment in Bedford. On it stood one of the baskets of blue flowers that she'd been given on the campaign trail that day. On the mantelpiece stood a card which someone in a South London police station had sent her. Its message said it all: 'Life is full of ups and downs . . .. But you're definitely an up.'

Mum unlocked one of her red boxes and pulled out the first folder. The job of Prime Minister is a lonely one, for loners.

WEEK THREE

Thursday, 2 June
7.00 a.m.: Breakfast with Chris Lawson, the Conservative
Party's Director of Marketing, and formerly with Mars. Amid
the clatter of knives and forks in the canteen at Conservative
Central Office, we discussed the soft-/hard-sell and marketing
aspects of the election campaign.

Chris first worked with Mum back in 1977, when she was in
Opposition, but he got his current job as a result of a rather
rude letter he had once written to the former Party Chairman,
Lord Thorneycroft, about the Party's communications – or
rather the lack of them.

'And I thought, that's me and politics finished!' he
laughed.

In fact, the reverse happened. When Cecil Parkinson
became Chairman in 1981, he called Chris in and suggested
that he should work full-time for the Party until the current
general election. He was delighted, though his golf and garden
have both gone to seed.

As a marketing man who had worked with product, Chris
was in an ideal position to be able to make comparisons and
point out contrasts between selling products and selling
policies. In fact, he thinks there's very little difference between
the two, provided that they are really good policies. 'I think
probably the only difference with policies is that once you are
in Government, you have much less say in what goes into
them.'

I started the ball rolling by asking him about the concept of
selling oneself to the electorate, which has been until recently

91

a peculiarly un-British thing to do. For ages the Conservative Party campaigns were terribly bland.

Chris reckoned that the new concepts came in with the decline of the hustings. Television was probably to blame for this, as people now won't go out and knock on doors to canvas as they want to stay home and watch the television. Nor will they bother to go to meetings to listen to politicians. Only when well-known politicians – ministers or opposition leaders – are billed to appear do meetings get support, and even then there is nothing near the level of audience there once was. So other means of communicating have had to be found.

Chris pointed out that one of the resultant problems of the domination by television is that it is organized by someone, else. Thus television and the press are perforce edited communications. 'Now the ministers, and the Prime Minister herself, and other members of the Party find it difficult sometimes to get through that editorial system the exact message they want to get across.'

The answer to this problem is to sell the Party to the media by developing your own media communications. Chris, in his early days at Central Office, found that the Conservative Party was producing a lot of literature, but that it wasn't well co-ordinated; it was going through all the various departments and constituencies and looked as if the Central Office was working for fifty different organizations. 'That's when the idea of the corporate identity symbol began to be important. I did feel quite strongly about the use of identity and ensuring that people knew where things were coming from.'

We then started to talk about the red, white and blue Olympic-style flame logo which I have described earlier. It is used on writing paper, stickers and all Party literature, as well as featuring strongly at political meetings and rallies. There have been Tory logos before, ranging from lions carrying flags to leopards changing their spots, but this time Chris felt that the symbol chosen should mean something to people. A designer was therefore commissioned to go round constituencies and various parts of the Party, like the National Union and the Young Conservatives, and ask the question: what does the Conservative Party mean to you – in one or two words, if possible?

Thirty constituencies' worth of research later, the designer had a list of words, including loyalty, leadership, willingness to work, and discipline. 'Now go away and come up with a design that will mean to us those words,' was his next instruction. Chris continued:

> He came up with this idea of the Olympic flame. Then he said, well, the Olympic flame means more than just that. It means the eternal flame, it means warmth, it means comfort, and that's how the concept of the flame developed.
>
> We had various attempts at design. Some flames had one, some two, some three, and some even four tongues. Some were pointed and looked vicious, others curved forwards, others backwards. So it wasn't just a matter of designing even a flame, it was a question of what shape flame we should choose.

The logo was duly launched at the 1982 Party Conference, and has proved a tremendous success.

'It's a very subtle logo, if you think about it,' Chris expanded. 'It wasn't just a case of getting a torch and saying, that's what we're carrying. It's much more subtle, because it has to satisfy an awful lot of demands, with people saying, "Oh, that's bad. Flames mean fire, which means fear," so we had to make it a friendly flame, and so on.'

Chris described as intangible the differences between marketing an opposition trying to get in to win, and a government attempting to win a second term.

> I think the differences are that when you're in Opposition (I wasn't working for the Conservatives then, because I was in the States), you spend most of your time knocking what the other party is doing and destroying what they're trying to do, or say they're trying to do. When you're in Government, at least you've got a record to go by, saying what you've done in the past, as well as what you're going to do in the future.
>
> That's why I think some of the criticisms that have been levelled at our Manifesto have proved totally

ineffective. One has been that it doesn't say anything different. Well, that is exactly right – we're not going to do anything different. 1983 has been a soft-sell campaign, unlike the hard-sell one that we conducted in 1979.

I then asked him about Saatchi & Saatchi, and their slogans, advertising, newspaper ads and party politicals. At the last general election they were generally credited with producing the images that were put across both of Mum and of the Conservative Party.

I think they probably had a bigger part to play then because of circumstances. Mrs Thatcher is now better known, as are her ministers. Thus Saatchi & Saatchi are a very major part of the operation, but they are only part of it. I think that if one takes the party political broadcasts, which we do in combination with them, they are the vehicle, if you like, through which a message is got across. Their creative department does work very closely with us in developing our own opinion research programme, which is extensive. Working from that opinion research, we can discern the level of lack of understanding of our policy and then we can work out target groups to get the message across. Then Saatchi & Saatchi's advertising – whether it's in the press, or our poster programme – is developed according to that.

I asked Chris to expand on the target groups:

Target groups are, of course, the first-time voters, the young housewives, C1s, C2s, skilled technicians, and the older people – they've always been very strongly Conservative – but the other groups have moved with us too. The 1979 election showed that we had secured the vote of forty-two per cent of young people. In the intervening years we lost a number of these, so one of the things we had to do was to direct quite a lot of attention to the young people.

We ended the discussion by looking at the way the election campaign had been staged:

> The first phase in the campaign is to attack the major opposition party. We started off meaning to hit very hard at the Labour Party Manifesto, which we did. We then watched very carefully where we were in the polls, a tactical week looking at how best to use our resources. In fact, we gained five points in the first ten days of the campaign. We could then see where we were going. For instance, during the early part of this week, we thought the National Health Service was going to prove a major problem for us because of what Healey and the others were saying. So we decided to answer their allegations not in the press or by advertisements, but through ministers and your mother. She did a tremendous job in the 'Panorama' programme.
>
> Next week, from today onwards, we go on to the attack again and get our own points across. We will combine positive policies and anti-Alliance material from now on. The Alliance has been a totally unknown quantity, and we still don't think anyone knows what is going to happen. In earlier campaigns we have known where we were all the time, but with a third party with various strengths throughout the country, it's very difficult to tell. One thing we do know is that whatever the other two parties do, as long as we stay above a certain level of poll, they will find it very difficult to move us off a very strong majority.

The campaign, according to Chris, had gone exactly as planned. But he didn't specify whether it was good planning or good fortune that was responsible.

But, weren't we giving an illusion of just coasting because everything seemed to be going the Conservative way, I queried?

'Totally untrue,' he countered. 'All good machinery sounds as though it's not making much noise.'

In front of us, ironically, lay the first day when 'Thatcher

Tours" itinerary didn't go entirely according to plan. The
East Midlands was our destination, with the aim of supporting candidates in the three Leicester constituencies. There is
currently a Labour majority of two thousand eight hundred
and fifty-six in Leicester East and one thousand nine hundred
and ninety-eight in Leicester South, which makes them both
potentially winnable marginals.

We flew up and joined the campaign bus, with our first
whistlestop in Shepshed. This is in the constituency of
North-West Leicestershire, a new seat created from the old
Bosworth and Loughborough constituencies.

Mum made a short speech through a loud hailer, supporting her candidate, David Ashby. Then she plunged into the
crowd. Such stops are becoming less like the jovial-talking,
handshaking walkabouts which characterized the early stages
of the campaign. Instead, they are strenuous exercises with a
greater volume of people, much jostling, and shouting to be
heard from Mum. This makes every one of them that much
more demanding.

A rally in Leicester Town Hall Square was followed by
another speech, and then we were on our way to the
ubiquitous factory visit. This time it was a knitwear factory,
manufacturing amongst other things sweaters for both Marks
& Sparks and the Ministry of Defence.

It was raining and gloomy as we left. There were gathering
clouds inside the bus too. Mum became increasingly anxious
about the programme, which was looking heavier every day.
Roger Boaden, Michael Spicer and David Wolfson went
through the schedule with her, but the expression on her face
indicated how she felt about the intensity of the next few days.

In addition, she was getting uptight about 'TV Eye' and
her interview with Alistair Burnet, which she was taping in
the evening to go on air later that night.

Ron Sharp, the driver of the campaign bus, at least
provided a distraction, though not a particularly happy one.
He suddenly slammed on the brakes, producing the first
drama of the afternoon. Briefcases and baskets of flowers shot
forwards, papers decanted themselves, and Alison Ward
found her typewriter hurtling off the desk to make heavy
contact with the floor. The subsequent crash suggested

terminal damage to the machine. When we picked it up and inspected it, we found, indeed, that it wasn't campaign-proof and had suffered rather badly.

Because of our stop-start slow progress through rainy Leicestershire, Mum was beginning to get anxious about the time as we fell further and further behind schedule.

At Market Harborough, where a large crowd had gathered to greet her, she decided that it would be quicker to continue in her car rather than the lumbering bus. The changeover proved the next hazard. Her car departed and, as we happily followed it out of town, it drew smartly away.

The awful truth dawned. We had no way of knowing which of the four missing members of our bus – viz, Mum, Dad, Derek Howe and Michael Spicer – had got into the Prime Minister's car, or the following back-up vehicle, or worse still, had been left behind in the crowded farewell from Market Harborough.

Roger Boaden looked ominous about the turn of events. We had, he pointed out, no police on board, no radio, and therefore no contact with the lead car. We had definitely lost our Leader.

It was unfortunate that Roger had just finished telling me the story of how, during the 1970 campaign, when Ted Heath was Leader, the campaign tour suffered the mishap of getting totally lost in Southampton. This was due to the fact that all the drivers in the convoy came from Bournemouth. On that occasion, harassed members of Mr Heath's staff were seen to turn up at a venue just as the Leader was emerging, having delivered his speech.

This day was one of anniversaries. Thirty years ago, Queen Elizabeth was crowned – on a similarly rainy day – and Everest was finally conquered. Twenty-five years ago, Roger Boaden started organizing his first political campaign. But Fate was not going to allow 2 June 1983 to be a day of rejoicing. We seemed about to add to the tally of campaign disasters. No one on board the bus knew the location of the Weetabix factory – our next stop. Alison, using the maps affixed to the back of our briefing to indicate the new constituency boundary changes, navigated us to Kettering, Weetabix's home town.

Then we had a stroke of luck. While casting around for more clues as to the exact whereabouts of this cereal factory, we spotted ahead of us a sunshine yellow Weetabix lorry. 'Follow that lorry,' ordered Alison, awarding herself eleven out of ten for initiative.

So, the campaign bus fell into the slipstream of the yellow lorry, emblazoned with 'Weetabix Wholemeal Cereal' across its rear. We followed, fervently hoping that it wasn't heading for Dover or an endless delivery round. Over the brow of the hill, and bingo: 'Look at all those yellow lorries. We're here,' someone yelled with delight.

But it was particularly quiet. The wrong Weetabix factory? No, the right one, but the back entrance. We were redirected round to the front, where the tell-tale line of demonstrators indicated a Prime Ministerial presence.

I never managed actually to get inside. Mum, who had also been delayed by the immovable obstacle of a mobile home blocking the road, had decided to make Weetabix a whistle-stop. A speedy look at how the place manages to produce three million Weetabix a day, and we left for the helicopter.

Back in Downing Street – fortunately without any more mishaps – Mum had her hair done, her make-up applied, and was briefed for her interview with Alistair Burnet for 'TV Eye'.

The programme was filmed downstairs in Number Twelve Downing Street, the Government Whip's Office. The interview was held in an elegant panelled room adjacent to the one where in 1805 the naval and military heroes of the Napoleonic Wars, Nelson and the Duke of Wellington, met for the first and only time.

Number Twelve used to be Number Thirteen, but when Numbers Eleven and Twelve were amalgamated to form the present home of the Chancellor of the Exchequer, they were all moved up a number. That's why there is a spare front door, boarded up, in between the famous front doors of Numbers Ten and Eleven.

Dad and I watched the recording, along with Gordon Reece. It went well, and Mum's reaction upstairs afterwards was one of relief. Basically she had adopted an approach of one-more-telly-appearance-down, three-more-to-go.

Looking a winner. The Prime Minister waves at Instrumental
Colour Systems in Newbury

The Conservative bandwagon being towed by tractor towards
Stoneleigh Abbey, Warwickshire. Ian Gow holds the umbrella
on the left, Mum waves to the passing throng, while Dad is
again immersed in political debate

Above: Mum's hair has just been done, but the expression on her face indicate: that the votes have yet to be counted

Above right: Red roses, a cake, a giant-sized card, and a thumbs-up sponge ar among the good luck messages on our hall table

Left: Chef and under chef in our flat at Number Ten, alias Crawfie, David Wolfson's secretary, and myself prepar ing dinner on polling night

Right: Polling night: the long wait for results begins with a family drink at Number Ten

'Margaret Hilda Thatcher has been duly elected to serve as a
Member of Parliament for the aforesaid constituency'

Screaming Lord Sutch of the Official Monster Raving Loony
Party raises his red topper victoriously, even though he polled
only 235 votes

As Mum proposes her vote of thanks after the declaration,
David Webb of the Anti-Censorship Party stages his own
declaration

Inside, looking down: my picture from the first-floor window of
Number Ten Downing Street. Mum, Dad and the media see in
the dawn of Mum's second term

Hurry up, Mum, I've got my diary to write. I wait in Number Ten for Mum's return from Central Office

A winning wave from a window o Conservative Central Office, Smit Square

Britain's first scientific Prime Minister, first woman Prime Minister and now first Conservative Prime Minister this century to win a second consecutive term of office, returns to Number Ten

Although she won't watch herself on television, or even play back the tape, she doesn't mind discussing what she replied to which question, nor whether she had done it as well as she should have.

Supper was followed by more speech-writing for the next day's rally in Birmingham. 'Page thirty-four, clear, page thirty-six, strike out. . . .' Mum was deep in concentration with the speech-writers when I took a tray of coffee in to them. Party Chairman, Cecil Parkinson, arrived just as we were watching him on Sir Robin Day's 'Question Time', the programme on which Denis partially backed down from his 'glorying in slaughter' remarks of the previous day.

The Falklands had dominated the day's media, and there had been almost unanimous disgust against Healey's outburst. David Owen had said, 'To talk of Mrs Thatcher glorying in Falklands slaughter is to move from the politics of the gutter to the politics of the abattoir.'

Before Mum settled down to her red boxes, we talked

The Standard, 2 June

"We shall fight in the gutters, we shall fight in the drains . . . !"

London Express Service/The Standard

briefly about Healey's attack and Labour's demand for an investigation into the sinking of the Argentine cruiser, *General Belgrano*.

I detected both a certain amount of bitterness and of astonishment in her voice, as she said: 'They have the luxury of knowing we came through all right, I had the anxiety of protecting our people on *Hermes* and *Invincible*, and the people on the vessels going down there.'

It was in exactly the same room that we were sitting in now, that I vividly remembered the scenes in the small hours, night after night, and the strain that she faced during the Falklands conflict, when a phone ringing or a knock at the door could mean a messenger bearing bad news: HMS . . . . . . hit by Exocet, casualties unknown.

Friday, 3 June
This day got off to an unexpectedly windy start for one television crew and a completely farcical one for the Prime Minister, all because our helicopter landed in the wrong field at Stoneleigh Abbey in Warwickshire.

Attempting to land, our twelve-seater chopper almost flattened a BBC camera crew with its powerful rotor wash. We then aborted the landing, gained height and circuited to look for an alternative site on which to put down.

While the BBC recovered from its close shave the Prime Minister, now on the ground, was encountering problems of a different nature. Outside the helicopter the wet grass was ankle deep – plainly unsuitable for her inside-only, high-heeled, suede court shoes.

I leapt out, grabbed the suitcase out of the back, rummaged around, and produced a stouter pair of shoes for her to change into. Now attired in more sensible footwear, Mum, followed by Dad and Ian Gow, climbed aboard a tractor-pulled, poster-covered farm trailer which was doubling as the platform.

What happened next was positively comical. The Conservative Party campaign's leading lady, her consort and her Parliamentary Private Secretary, all sheltering from the drizzle under multi-coloured golfing umbrellas, bumped across a damp meadow in totally the opposite direction from the crowd which was waiting to welcome them.

This was obviously going to be a countrified whistlestop at a relaxed rural tempo. Some minutes later, after their cross-country journey, the VIPs came into view and halted in front of the small crowd.

Now looking especially festive in a Sikh garland, Mum spoke for a few moments before the crowd, the Press and she all gratefully got in out of the rain.

On board the campaign bus, we set off for the rest of our West Midlands electioneering tour. Our objective: any winnable marginal in the Coventry and Birmingham areas.

Mum was not happy with events. No one, it transpired, had mentioned to her that the rally at Stoneleigh Abbey was an open air one, or that she had to speak, or that the press would be there.

The day showed every sign of emulating the previous one, with a saga of things going wrong. The first mishap was a missing press release about the unemployment figures, which Mum found in her handbag after there had been much searching through files and briefcases.

A batten-down-the-hatches attitude was prevailing on the bus. At a Coventry hotel, Mum gave media interviews and had lunch with regional editors. Meanwhile, Tessa, Alison and I had lunch with the press and discovered that their day hadn't got off to a great start either. They felt that they were being given insufficient Prime Ministerial attention and had composed a protest song to the tune of 'Daisy, Daisy'.

> Maggie, Maggie, give us an interview,
> We're all crazy to have a word with you.
> We don't need a lot of copy,
> But Maggie, we're gonna get stroppy
> If you don't, toute suite,
> Get to your feet,
> And give us a par' or two.

> Maggie, Maggie, give us an interview,
> Your not speaking's making us all feel blue.
> You talk to the guys from the telly,
> But to us – not on your nelly.

So please relax,
And give the hacks
A minute or two, with you.

Maggie, Maggie, speak to us, Maggie do,
We've got questions we'd like to put to you.
We know that you think us a menace,
And reptiles – according to Denis.
But really we're sweet,
So why don't we meet,
Just give us an interview.

As Maggie was scheduled to give them a briefing that evening, at least one problem looked as though it was on the way to being solved.

But everything wasn't running with its usual smoothness yet. Two eggs splattered down the side of the bus as we arrived at Aston Science Park in Birmingham. That unfriendly reception was continued inside when Councillor Clive Wilkinson, a board member and leader of Birmingham Council's Labour Group – who had already had the red carpet taken up in protest of Mum's visit – told her that he resented her trying to make political gain and get kudos from her visit to the park.

The kerfuffle prompted one remark which put this ludicrous episode into perspective. '*You're* not being political, of course,' a voice in the crowd chipped in. Nothing daunted, Mum toured the Science Park, which promotes the development of new high tech' business.

A stimulating and successful visit to the *Birmingham Mail*'s .Ideal Home Exhibition at the National Exhibition Centre revived the day. Visitors deserted the attractions of the five fully-furnished luxury homes and 220 stands to crane their necks and strain to get a glimpse of the surprise VIP in their midst. Crowds three or four deep lined the blue carpet which was acting as the Prime Ministerial walkway.

Mum, thoroughly enjoying the occasion, shook hands, signed autographs and talked to children – some of whom were sitting on their parents' shoulders to get a better view – old people and families.

'Who is creating all the fuss?' a man asked me when I was loitering on the fringes of the crowd.

'The Prime Minister,' I replied.

Mum was something of a surprise to another couple. 'I thought she was taller than that,' remarked one to the other.

'What's she up to?' I enquired of one onlooker.

'She's pretending to be interested in some spastic child,' he replied.

'Why pretending?' I countered.

'Well, she can't be interested if she takes that much out of the National Health Service.'

I was tempted to reel off the Conservative track record on the social services, but had to get out of the way in the face of her advance.

Some didn't fancy the scrum and, noticing the television lights and paraphernalia, wisely decided that they'd wait until later to find out what all the razza-matazz was about – in the comfort of their sitting-room sofas.

'Don't bother,' I heard one man say to his wife, who was making moves to get a bit closer, 'We'll see it on the news tonight.'

This, I suppose, strengthens the argument that election campaigns these days are all television affairs.

A look inside one of the furnished houses resembled being in a goldfish bowl, with Mum admiring the fixtures and fittings, while fellow visitors to the exhibition pressed their faces to the windows to look in.

Eventually it was decided that we should go out by the back door, so we headed for the exit, gathering momentum as we went. I raced at a brisk trot past one man on the wine stand. He was standing, bottle in hand, about to present it to Mrs T. I assumed. She whizzed past so fast that I just caught him commenting, 'Not a chance' and taking two steps backwards to avoid being run over.

Mum was buoyed up by the enthusiasm of the people she'd talked to. Their warmth and support had been inspiring to watch. The faces which lit up, and the voices willing her on, said a lot about the feeling in this election campaign.

'That was much better, we met some people,' Mum declared back on the bus, collapsing onto a seat.

Someone outside passed in two pieces of paper with a request for autographs. Mum obliged, producing a felt-tipped pen to sign with.

'Oh, for God's sake,' started Dad. 'Come on love, no,' he pleaded. He knew only too well that if you start signing autographs, the floodgates open, and you're stuck signing away for ages.

'We either sign autographs or meet people, today we're meeting the people,' he'll quite often say when pens, pencils and scraps of paper are pushed towards him.

This campaign has been really good for him. Because he is now so recognizable, he often skirts round the outside of the crowds and chats up people who won't have a hope of getting a glimpse of Mum through the throng.

'Ooh look, there's Denis,' is a familiar cry from people who spot him, and he goes over and exudes merry *bonhomie* to the old, the young, males and females. Frank Johnson, in *his* campaign trail diary in *The Times*, has judged Dad's mastery of the factory-visit conversation as the equal of the Duke of Edinburgh's. High praise indeed.

A few hours in the Metropole Hotel in Birmingham gave Mum the opportunity to get to grips with the speech for the night's rally. Chain munching biscuits and drinking tea, she went through the speech complaining that it didn't read very well, and that there were too few clap lines.

'Look, love, it'll be fine,' encouraged Dad, who has heard every possible whinge you can make about a speech over the years.

Over supper, I asked her how she though it was going. Her view, and her worry, is that people are sometimes too optimistic. She is a realist when it comes to campaigns. When it was suggested to her that she drop an engagement she refused, not wanting at any cost to be seen to be slacking. 'You can lose elections in the last few days by not going flat out to the winning post,' she said.

The speech, given in a hall in the Metropole Hotel, lasted fifty-seven minutes, which she said afterwards had been too long. I stood at the back of the hall, to make a change from sitting on the platform, and heard her spell out six reasons for voting Conservative on 9 June:

Because the Conservatives offer real hope of new jobs
Because the Conservatives keep prices down
Because the Conservatives reform trade union law
Because the Conservatives give council house tenants the chance to own their own home
Because the Conservatives protect the social services
Because the Conservatives ensure that this nation is properly defended

Afterwards we returned to London down the M1. 'How long will it take us to get from Coventry to London?' I asked the driver. 'You're in Birmingham,' he corrected me. I immediately understood how American politicians on the year-long Presidential trail perpetually get their whereabouts wrong. Here was I doing it after only two weeks.

Saturday, 4 June

'Give me a call if I show signs of sleeping in in the morning,' I'd asked Mum the previous night, on discovering that my alarm clock had broken. But, I hadn't anticipated her interpreting this as, 'wake me up at dawn'. It was 5.55 a.m. when my lie-in was interrupted by a Prime Ministerial alarm call – in person at the end of my bed!

Later, as Mum was having her hair permed before we set off to canvass London marginals, we talked about provisional plans for next weekend. There is absolutely nothing like an election to instil a sense of insecurity and uncertainty in a household, however positive the pointers towards victory may be.

Quite simply, a giant-sized question mark hangs over everything after Thursday. There are win or lose options to every plan. I've delayed stocking up the freezer in case we have to move everything out in a hurry. Friends who have asked me to do things either on Friday or at the weekend have received non-committal answers because, if the polls are totally wrong, we just might all be flinging belongings into a packing case.

Next weekend, for instance, if we have won Mum and Dad

will probably go to Chequers. If we've lost they will be off to Scotney, our flat in Kent.

We face a dilemma, too, about Trooping the Colour (the actual performance proper, as opposed to all the rehearsals with which we've been serenaded), which takes place next Saturday. Mum traditionally gives a buffet lunch for guests who have watched the Birthday Parade from seats in the Prime Minister's stand outside Number Ten. As Polling Day is in between now and then we can't ask anyone until we know that we will still be here. As a compromise, we arranged that the girl who will have to cook the lunch should be put or stand-by and the guests will have to be last-minute invitees.

'We don't count our chickens until they hatch,' is one of Mum's much-used phrases, referring to anything post-9 June.

Unlike the Civil Servants in various anonymous high-rise office blocks around town, who have been making contingency plans for a change of government, so that they can advise a new one how to implement its manifesto, we have not made any moving plans.

Number Ten or, more accurately, the government machinery within it, lives in a kind of no man's land during election campaigns. The Prime Minister's Office, which consists of five private secretaries and the Principal Private Secretary, Robin Butler, just ticks over while the electorate makes up its mind who will be the next occupant of Number Ten. The private office's workload is drastically cut and on some days it is manned by only two rather than the normal strength of five private secretaries.

Parliament isn't sitting at the moment, nor is internal government business being generated, so just about the only Prime Ministerial duties are foreign policy matters, correspondence or statistics, such as the unemployment figures.

According to Robin Butler, this has been a very quiet election campaign from the Prime Ministerial viewpoint because nothing major has blown up. A couple of the issues which have required the private office doing some work have been the Labour Party's leaked documents allegations and accusations about the sinking of the *Belgrano*.

Mum's red boxes have contained only a quarter of their usual contents. The week before Polling Day, the private office starts working on the possibility of a new boss if the present Government is defeated, or cranking the machine up to get back to business as normal. The latter option means that if Mum wins on Friday the private office can aid her to make an early reshuffle if she so wishes, advise her of new Government business, and start preparing the Queen's Speech for the Opening of Parliament.

Eventually we left by car to go out to support three candidates in marginal London seats: John Wheeler in Westminster North, Harry Greenway in Ealing North and John Gorst in Hendon North. After a crowded but successful walkabout in St John's Wood High Street we clambered aboard the campaign bus.

We had left Number Ten on a bright, sunny summer's morning with the dress rehearsal of Trooping the Colour in full swing and, at last, it seemed as though we were on the final home stretch of the campaign.

Mum said little on the journey from Westminster North to Ealing North, preoccupied with the following day, which carried a heavy programme, and the rest of the campaign. We all glanced through the newspapers and enjoyed a pretty unpressurized spell of electioneering, taking our cue perhaps from the relaxed attitude of the Saturday morning shoppers that we were meeting.

Harry Greenway, outside his campaign headquarters in Greenford, turned on a model how-to-stage-manage an outdoor meeting. He had had the courtyard cordoned off with orange tape and bollards, which meant that so many more people could see Mum than would have been able to had they all squashed in towards her.

We were met by Mrs Greenway and their children, all sporting 'Vote for Daddy' centres in the blue rosettes. Mum spoke briefly and simply, then chatted to the crowd. Dad, after all his previous strictness, took signing an autograph rather seriously, purposefully striding off with pen and paper to find a car bonnet on which to press.

Back on the road again to Hendon North and another shopping walkabout. I skipped most of this one in order to do some genuine shopping. Mum and Dad then went on to

Finchley for an afternoon of campaigning in Mum's constituency.

Home again later, Mum started working on her speech for
the Youth Rally at Wembley the next day.

Opening my mail, I was touched by this letter from a
correspondent who signed himself 'contented OAP and
ex-RAF'.

> Good luck to our Prime Minister, not only on 9 June but
> in the years to come.
> Her grip, her zest, her stamina, all are remarkable by
> any standards.
> Her honesty sometimes obscures her abundant charm.
> Thank you for helping her.

After the 'hate mail' which frequently arrives, this letter
was a special one to read.

Later, John Selwyn Gummer, Ferdy Mount and David
Wolfson came up to the flat to work on the speech and for
supper. The latter was the usual hotchpotch – soup and salad
(produced by Crawfie, David Wolfson's secretary), fruit salad
(made by Mum's constituency secretary, Joy), and chicken
and cold sausages (my effort).

But they weren't the only people who were hungry. Alison
and Tessa, working furiously downstairs in the political office,
decided they were absolutely famished and that the answer
was to raid the Prime Minister's fridge. Up they went and
discovered an appetizing-looking joint of cold roast beef,
which Crawfie and Joy told them needed eating up. They
were poised, carving knife at the ready, when this little feast
was interrupted by the approach of the Prime Ministerial
dinner party. Anxious not to be caught scoffing in the kitchen,
they dropped the beef, platter and carving knife into the deep
knife drawer where they came to rest on top of knives, potato
peelers, skewers, tea strainers and other kitchen utensils.

They sloped off, relieved to have avoided detection.
Unfortunately, Dad walked out of the dining room looking for
a corkscrew, which also lives in the knife drawer. A startled,
'What the bloody hell is this?' was Dad's reaction to
happening upon the hidden cold roast. Hasty explanations

followed and Alison and Tessa were summoned up to consume supper in more legitimate and official circumstances.

The incident caused much laughter downstairs in the political office, where I was borrowing an electric typewriter to write this diary.

At midnight, Alison and Tessa were still attempting to decipher some hand-written amendments to the Wembley speech (neither Mum nor Ferdy has particularly legible scrawl). Whatever time Mum got to bed, they were in for an even later night.

Sunday, 5 June
The first bright spot of the day was the arrival of the Sunday papers shortly after midnight. Front page headlines in most of them predicted a Tory landslide on Thursday. *The Mail on Sunday* splashed across its front page, 'On Course for 260 majority'; the *News of the World*'s poll of women voters showed Tories 45 per cent, Alliance 28 per cent and Labour 24 per cent which prompted the headline, 'The Mums back Maggie – and push Labour into third place'. *The Sunday Times* forecasted the Tories heading for a 130-seat landslide and the *Sunday Express*'s poll in key marginals showed Conservatives 43½ per cent, Labour 31 per cent and Alliance 23½ per cent which inspired the headline writer to forecast Thursday's result as 'Mrs T by a mile say key voters'.

I passed Ian Gow in the corridor which leads to Number Ten's front door, and we agreed that it was a marvellous press. 'I hope people vote though,' I added.

I didn't see Mum until she appeared on the television, interviewed by Brian Walden on 'Weekend World' at noon. At present, she is so busy that the only indications that she still lives here are the phone messages I take from the front door to say that the hairdresser is on his way up, or that the TV make-up girl has arrived. Otherwise I leave out the occasional change of clothes, return the discarded ones to their rightful cupboards and catch a glimpse of her dashing down the stairs.

Dad and I watched 'Weekend World', which was recorded live from Number Twelve, together in the sitting room in the flat. Mum came over superbly and seemed now to have got the knack, however many tough questions were fast bowled at her, of hitting them for six.

'Brilliant', declared Dad at the end, racing down to her study to congratulate her. After seeing Anthony Shrimsley and Brian Walden in the study for a drink, they both returned upstairs for what turned out to be an exceptionally uncivilized Sunday lunch.

Families up and down the country were no doubt sitting down to the conventional Sunday lunch. But this was not at all the case in Number Ten. Here, the scenario was an example of eating on the job. At one stage, Mum was polishing off her pudding of chocolate ice cream, while flipping through her speech for the afternoon's Youth Rally at Wembley. Ian Gow, halfway through his smoked salmon sandwiches, was on the phone dictating changes in the speech to Alison, who was typing out the Autocue tape at Wembley.

David Wolfson had left the dining room altogether. His task was to get the quotes that Mum was using in the speech typed up. The relevant sections of the Labour Manifesto had to be transformed into large, readable type and fixed into the relevant page of 'The New Hope for Britain'. As he was departing, Mum cautioned David not to include the quotes from Rudyard Kipling – one of her favourite poets, whose lines she so often knows by heart – in the Manifesto as well.

Today was to prove a heavy one – all go: with the hour-long major television interview in the morning; a speech to two thousand five hundred Young Conservatives in the afternoon; and getting the last party political broadcast in the can in the evening.

The Youth Rally at Wembley Conference Centre promised to be something spectacular. During the 1979 election campaign Mum had spoken at a similar rally to an audience of trade unionists, and the atmosphere, according to all reports, had been absolutely electric.

This rally proved to be the same. Waiting backstage in the dark to be cued to go on, Mum, who gets a bit nervous about being 'outglittered' by show business personalities, turned, in a momentary attack of stage fright, and said, 'Oh, how I wish it was over'. Once on, she was greeted with cheers from the audience at a football-match decibel count level, and received a hyped-up rapturous ovation normally reserved for pop groups. But, this was pop politics. The choice of music varied from 'I can't let Maggie Go', to 'Congratulations'. Pop singer Lynsey de Paul had composed a song which she played and sang:

> Vote Tory, Tory, Tory
>   For election glory
> We don't want U-turns
>   So we'll vote for Maggie T.
> Vote Tory, Tory, Tory
>   The only party for me
> Say No to Labour
> And No to the SDP

Exactly the musical sentiments the audience thought it was there to hear.

The audience wore jeans, had long hair, sported t-shirts and were years younger than the people that had attended earlier rallies of this campaign. Huge signs held aloft indicated which part of the country they had come from. Stars from the stage, screen and sportsfield lent their own glamour to the event. Film director Bryan Forbes, and his actress wife, Nanette Newman, snooker champion Steve Davis, comedians Jimmy Tarbuck and Bob Monkhouse, disc jockey Kenny Everett, cricketer Fred Trueman, swimmer Sharron Davies, gymnast Susanne Dando, last year's Grand National winner Bob Champion, and film director Michael Winner were among the celebrities who were there to lend their support.

Trumpets and waving balloons welcomed Mum and a thunderous chant of 'Maggie, Maggie, Maggie, In, In, In' reached a crescendo as she bowed and waved. The audience had been warmed up by previous acts, one of which – Kenny Everett's – was to prove controversial. 'Let's bomb Russia', and 'Let's kick Michael Foot's stick away', he had joked. These jokes were to boomerang back with allegations of bad taste when the laughter had died away.

Mum spoke for thirty-five minutes and the boisterous applause was mind boggling. What this audience would have done had she arrived with a landslide victory to her name, Heaven only knows.

There was a touch of audience participation in her speech. 'Could Labour have managed a Rally like this?'

'No', two thousand five hundred voices roared back.

The Prime Minister produced her favourite speech asset – the Opposition's Manifesto. After she had read out an anti-sexist provision which proposed 'that job segregation within and outside the home is broken down', she joked that Labour was going to see that Denis did his fair share of the washing-up. That brought the house down and much laughter from Dad himself.

At the end, her exit was tantamount to a lap of honour, except she hadn't yet won. Ecstatic hands reached out to shake hers as she tried to cope with both sides of the aisles at once.

The atmosphere was of the sort usually found at film premieres at the Odeon in Leicester Square, with the

Daily Mail, 7 June

Associated Newspapers/Daily Mail

emphasis on razza-mattaz. In fact, just about the only thing missing was 007 himself, who was in town for the opening of the latest Bond offering, *Octopussy.*

At tea with the stars in the Champion Bar, I managed to score a public relations triumph. I had picked up off the stage an enormous foam-rubber glove in the shape of a thumbs-up sign, with 'Maggie's a Winner' written across it in blue letters.

Despite his protests – 'I'll look even more bloody silly than usual' – I persuaded Dad to wear it and to wave. The photograph appeared in several of the national dailies the following day and, via the Press Association, in about thirty-five provincial newspapers – a better achievement than the thousands of other photographs which have been taken in the last fortnight on this election trail and never reached the newspapers.

From Wembley, Mum went directly to the television studio to start work on the party political broadcast. Tim Bell of Saatchi & Saatchi, the Conservative Party's advertising agency for the second election running, and Gordon Reece were outside to meet her.

For this election Saatchi & Saatchi have produced five

Daily Express, 18 May

"How shocking of you, Mrs Thatcher, to conduct a smear campaign against us!"

London Express Service/Daily Express

party political broadcasts, four newspaper advertisements, seven radio broadcasts and three posters. The emphasis on party politicals, according to Tim, has been more serious than some of the flip elements which featured in 1979 broadcasts. For this election too, the other parties have also sought the services of advertising agencies to market themselves, their image and their policies more effectively. The Labour Party has turned to Johnnie Wright & Partners for help with advertising, while the Alliance have used Gold, Greenlees Trott Ltd.

I didn't go in to watch the recording, because the fewer hangers-on at occasions like this, the better. Instead, I went back to Number Ten and found a suit for Mum, which went round to the studio by car. This was for her to wear in case they got past rehearsals and actually shot something.

Mum later explained that she hadn't been happy with the script because its content wasn't original or punchy enough. She had worked on it to alter it and then, after only three takes, got the broadcast in the can, much to everyone's satisfaction, even if it did mean working very late into Sunday night.

I saw it on the video and felt that it came over superbly. It began with 'vox pops', with comments such as: 'She's good for the country and I think she won't take no nonsense, and she keeps to what she says – she carried it through and she doesn't change her mind halfway. I think you've got to give her another term because four years is not long enough'; and: 'I admire her enormously. I think that she's the first person that we have had in the government since the end of the war who is standing up for Britain.' These remarks immediately created the impression to the viewer that here was a lady who thinks positive and has the spunk to get on with the job.

Mum's piece to camera was a polished and convincing performance. She ended her speech on a high and commanding note: 'May I suggest to every citizen of our country, every man and every woman of whatever political persuasion, that on Thursday you pause and ask yourself one question – who would best defend our freedom, our way of life, and the much-loved land in which we live?

'Britain is on the right track. Don't turn back.'

The broadcast illustrated well a point that she had made to

me when I once asked her how she thought the job had changed her. She said then that a personality merges with the job, and gains an authority which is never lost. This came through loud and clear in this, her last party political broadcast of the campaign.

Monday, 6 June

It's Monday – it must be the marzipan manufacturers in Mitcham and Morden, one of two marginal London seats that Mum was scheduled to visit this morning. (The second was Croydon North-West.) Angela Rumbold had won the seat in a by-election in June 1982, following the resignation of ex-Labour MP, Bruce Douglas-Mann, who unsuccessfully sought a mandate as an SDP candidate. It's the Conservatives' seventh most marginal seat.

I skipped the visit to John F. Renshaw Ltd, the marzipan makers, not out of distaste for marzipan, but because I'd gone along to Conservative Central Office to talk to Gerry Mulligan. Gerry was the Office's chief press officer for the elections of 1974 and 1979. He has now retired, but was asked to come in and help out for this campaign as he is so experienced. I wanted to talk to him about how he saw the way the press were reporting the campaign, the personalities and the parties.

First, he explained to me how he organizes the 'dawn run'. He starts leafing through the next day's papers at about 10.30 p.m., and by one in the morning he has got Central Office more or less to himself. He then settles down to the near-impossible task of compressing information from about three hundred pages of newspapers into five sheets of A4 typing. Once he has done this, he wanders over to Number Ten at about 5.30 a.m. with the result. His role is to ensure that the Prime Minister is acquainted with all the items of information that she needs for her daily morning press conference.

I began our interview by asking him for some general observations on the newspaper coverage: 'The press consensus in 1979 was heavily in favour of Mrs Thatcher. The consensus today is even more heavily in her favour.'

Gerry then started to consider the way that individual papers were looking at the election:

> The *Daily Star*, for example, which so far as I can detect started out backing the Labour Party, seems now if not actually backing the Conservatives, at least to be inclined towards them. That is possibly the one switch that I see in Fleet Street. Of course, *The Guardian* and the *Daily Mirror* seem to be as anti-Conservative as ever. But the latter has been denied any material with which to support the Labour Party, so that when these terrible gaffs are made, the poor *Daily Mirror* has to put them down column on page five. They have got nothing to get their teeth into on behalf of the Labour Party.

I asked him if he thought the papers had set out to treat this election rather differently from previous ones – I had been struck by the number of what might be called trivial stories on peripheral matters. He didn't think there was any deliberate change in emphasis, but did say that Fleet Street were disappointed because it seemed to be a one-horse race. 'Now

Daily Telegraph, 4 June

"And in the final straight its Thatcher on Landslide from-er-um . . ."

Patrick Garland/Daily Telegraph

in previous elections, in my experience – and I have seen a lot of them – there has always been an element of doubt as to the result. And that, of course, makes it far more interesting to Fleet Street. We have got to the rather regrettable stage where you can't even have a bet on the General Election. First of all William Hill stopped all bets, and now Ladbrookes have followed suit.'

I wanted to know, in that case, which General Election he did rate as the most exciting from a press point of view:

> That is a difficult one because my memory is getting hazy. I suppose the most exciting was when Churchill defeated Attlee in 1951, and the whole thing was in doubt until about four o'clock on the Friday afternoon following the poll. I forget what Churchill's majority was, but it was very, very slender.
>
> The 1979 election was exciting for the world because, of course, you had Mrs Thatcher as potentially the first woman Prime Minister of an advanced industrialized Western country, and the great question was, 'Can she do it?' Now today the excitement of a lady Prime Minister has gone because she has already established the fact for the last four years.

We then turned to the headlines that have appeared during the campaign. Gerry didn't think they had been particularly memorable, though *The Sun's* judgment of the Labour Party as THIRD RATE, as a result of their slippage in the opinion polls, will stand as the most dramatic. He reckoned that the Labour Party will change in character after the election, and this election will mark the end of the Party as we know it.

He considered that some of the newspaper writing had been brilliant, particularly in the popular papers like the *Daily Mail, The Sun* and the *Daily Express*, where ideas have to be put over in fifty words where some people would take five hundred to say the same thing. The cartoons, too, he liked, observing that most of them seemed pro-Tory.

I asked him what he thought of the way the press have treated the SDP:

I would say they have treated them pretty fairly, but what I have noticed is that the newspapers in the first week or ten days tended to pat them on the head like a small boy. But, of course, you don't expect that small boy to grow up very quickly. Now the press have seen that the Alliance is not a small boy, and that it will expand into a teenager. And a teenager who can be strong enough possibly to knock down an adult one day. So, they are taking them more seriously.

The Alliance were slow in getting moving early in the campaign. It would seem that the fault lay with Roy Jenkins, and the public still look to Roy Jenkins as the leader, although Steel is supposed to be in charge of the campaign. That may well have been quite a major mistake on the part of the SDP.

Finally, I asked Gerry if he believed in last-minute changes: 'Oh yes, I do. Harold Wilson in 1970 (I think) was given a lead and lost. Certainly – and this is purely hypothetical – some dreadful thing could happen at this very moment, or because of television or the press there could be a great mass of publicity rushing on the public, and their minds could be changed in just half an hour.'

The marzipan factory, judging from comments by Alison, Tessa and company, when they came back later, had been action packed. For a start, Ron had reversed the campaign bus a bit too near an overhanging roof and snapped off the radio TV aerial, while Alison at her desk was in mid phone call.

Once inside the factory, a BBC man was heard to complain about being taken to a nut house, while Dad blithely asked, 'What do you do with the nuts here?', which, taken out of context . . . .

Everyone seemed to have learnt something about marzipan, which most of us know only as the glue between the icing and the Christmas cake, or the choice of chocolate centre usually left at the bottom of the box. This is how Frank Johnson of *The Times* saw the Prime Ministerial tour of the almond delicacy in the making:

Keeping voters sweet with the gut issues

One of the happiest moments of Mrs Thatcher's election campaign of 1979 was her visit to the Cadbury's factory in a Birmingham marginal.

There, balancing on the brink of successive vats of whirling chocolate, with the crush of photographers threatening to propel her downward at any moment, she narrowly missed being incorporated in a range of delicious walnut whips. The history of Britain over the last four years could have been so different.

Many of us interpreted that visit as the turning point of the 1979 campaign – there being more pigs among the electorate than joggers.

Yesterday, just over four years later, she kept faith with the pivotal 'fat vote' by visiting a marzipan factory in a south London marginal.

'11.00 a.m. Arrive John F. Renshaw Ltd, Lock Lane, Mitcham Manufacturers of Marzipan', said the sheet of paper issued to those of us travelling with the Prime Minister. 'Please note: very limited press facilities because of hygiene regulations'.

This was rather offensive, since some of us reporters are a good deal less filthy than some politicians.

Three coaches, one of them containing the Prime Minister, descended on the factory. Then, as in Act Two of *The Nutcracker*, we children were led by her through the Kingdom of Sweets.

The elegant Mr Denis Thatcher was characteristically reliable in the role of the Prince. The photographers were of course the rats. Opinions will differ as to whether the Prime Minister was dancing the role of the Sugar Plum Fairy or the Wicked Fairy.

Balletomanes will note that, if it was the Wicked Fairy rather than the Sugar Plum Fairy then the ballet must have been *The Sleeping Beauty* because *The Nutcracker* does not have a Wicked Fairy, so it would be best if this balletic metaphor were abandoned. Anyway, there were a lot of sweets.

The machinery clattered. The marzipan churned and gurgled. Women continued to stuff chunks of it into brown boxes. Mrs Thatcher started to make full use of her gift of being piercingly interested in whatever is being explained to her on an election tour.

Unlike the sadly limited Mr Foot, she has many roles which, depending on the role of the person whom she is addressing, she can assume at will – politician, wife, mother, shopper, marzipan-maker.

On this occasion she was all five. 'Making marzipan with almonds is a brute of a job', she told a group of the women, referring to her own experience of the process.

Meanwhile Mr Denis Thatcher, whose mastery of factory-visit conversation is now the equal of the Duke of Edinburgh's, could be heard in the background working away at the firm's executives: 'Do you buy your almonds from the almond people overseas? . . . I see, yes . . . you make the cherries, d'you?' Back to the Prime Minister, still working the women. 'I don't like too much of it because it is VAIRY, VAIRY rich . . . .'

Clatter-clatter, continued the machines. Gurgle-gurgle, continued the marzipan. The Prime Minister sat down at a conveyor belt with some more women and joined in the sorting of dark almonds from light. Whereupon, the photographers started climbing up the adjacent walls, and indeed each other.

'By law, you can only make marzipan with almonds,' an executive was at the same time explaining to Mrs Thatcher, which is in itself an astonishing piece of information.

Excitement mounted. 'You skin them and grind them yourself,' the Prime Minister could be heard bafflingly telling some of the executives at one stage. This turned out to be a further reference to her way with nuts, when marzipan-making, rather than to her way with Cabinet colleagues.

A joyous occasion, then. Sadly it was time to go.

Reluctantly, we took off the long white coats, and the white hats, which all of us – including the Prime Minister – had had to wear for hygiene reasons.

Mr Thatcher had looked in his like a reassuring

surgeon in a private hospital catering for senior business-men.

'Nothing wrong with a medium sherry now and then, old boy,' one could imagine him advising after an op. 'But I'd go easy on stuff like marzipan if I were you.'

Tuesday, 7 June

The campaign climax – our last rally in Fleetwood in Lancashire, had a jubilant end of campaign air about it. Mum had opted for the basic barn-storming approach to her speech – speaking from notes – and so had dispensed with both the Autocue and the formal script.

This meant an avoidance of the fraught hours of panic that had taken place in hotel rooms up and down the country before all previous rallies, as last-minute amendments and changes were made to the speech.

It was, therefore, up to each team member, according to his or her own inclination, to decide how to fill the forty-five minutes before we were due to leave the North Euston Hotel, Fleetwood, for the Marine Hall, a short distance along the front.

Alison and Tessa rejoiced, 'The strife is o'er, the typing done.' I learnt from Derek Howe, at length, his complicated and comprehensive method of winning bets on the election results. He was spreading his money on an overall majority of between 120 and 150 odd seats, which I thought was a bit optimistic, but I bowed to his better judgment. In fact, as Derek has made a profit on his election punting at every election since 1970, I have paid close attention, in the hope of making a pound or two.

Along the corridor, Dad and David Wolfson were to be found closeted in a room, glued to a colour television. In progress was a fierce contest of rugger between the All Blacks and the Lions. David was benefiting from an extra commentary from Dad, who used to be a rugby football referee.

They looked up, and chorused guiltily in tandem, 'You won't put this in your book, will you?'

'Yes,' I answered sternly, 'but, of course, you've just changed channels while monitoring the election coverage . . . .'

There was no sign whatsoever of Roger Boaden and John Whittingdale. A search located them in the bar downstairs, shoving money into a fruit machine . . . . The end of the campaign cometh.

In a packed Marine Hall, where the temperature must have been at sauna level, Mum told the audience that this was a landmark election: 'It's a result that will reverberate through our history. Its consequences will outlive most of us here tonight.'

From my position, standing at one side, I noticed that large numbers of the audience were looking distinctly uncomfortable because of the heat. Sweaty photographers wandered out for air and cooling-off intermissions. The captive audience of the faithful had no such chance, and some resorted to fanning themselves, as the deafening claps of a humid thunderstorm crashed overhead. I wondered how on earth one lady, clad in a pink-petalled hat and fur coat, hadn't evaporated.

At the end of the meeting, Mum was presented with a bag of fish caught by Morecambe Bay fishermen, and held one up for the benefit of photographers. A request for an encore followed, and so she delved into the bottom of the carrier bag and, in the style with which conjurors pull white rabbits out of their black hats, retrieved a lengthy piece of haddock and held it up . . . amid more cheers.

Near disaster threatened Alison, Tessa and myself on our return trip to the airport, Warton Aerodrome, at Preston, where we had landed. We were the lead car in the convoy when, without warning, the police escort turned around and deserted us. He was also doubling, of course, as the navigator.

'Have you any idea where the airport is?' we enquired anxiously of the driver, foreseeing major problems. 'Looks like it's up the promenade, we can't go wrong.' Famous last words.

We took the scenic route along the entire Blackpool front. It was my inaugural visit to Blackpool, and the famous resort passed in a grey blur in the pouring rain, punctuated by flashes of dramatic lightning.

We passed under the much-famed, but tonight unlit, Blackpool illuminations. Alison and Tessa were veterans of Tory Party conferences which for years were held in this venue of venues. They provided the running commentary on this conducted tour, as this was nostalgic territory for them both. As they reminded one another of back-stage dramas at various party conferences during the 1970s, of who got drunk, and of who went swimming, etc, we passed by the palatial hotels in which such junketings took place. We began to cease worrying about where Mum might be, whether she had arrived at the airport already, and whether we'd ever get there in time ourselves.

At the airport we grabbed briefcases and clobber out of the back of the car and made a dash for the plane steps. On board we found Mum ensconsed with a drink in relaxed form and high spirits.

She said that making her speech that night had been difficult, thanks to the crashes with which she had to cope, not knowing whether they were from demonstrators breaking through something, an aeroplane going through the sound barrier, or a clap of thunder.

'Where are our coach friends?' she enquired, coining a new name for the reptiles. On a pub' crawl, someone suggested. When they duly arrived, Mum ordered a round of applause from the front section of the plane.

Mum and I chatted about Sir Robin Day's 'Election Call', the radio and television programme that she had broadcast first thing in the morning. She often asks me how I think her radio/television programmes have gone, as I worked in television in Australia for two years. I told her how astonished I was that she looked an exact replica of her 1979 campaign photograph after four years in office, which would have knackered most people.

After a moment's hesitation at the beginning, while she realized that she wasn't going to be able to see the callers, only hear them on the telephone, it went well – although she thought that some of the questioners rambled on far too long. There was one particularly nice, light, humorous moment when she apologized to Sir Robin for having called him plain Mister all through the 'Panorama' programme.

Eleven questions from around the country homed in on a variety of topics, including one person who objected to Kenny Everett's jokes at Sunday's Youth Rally at Wembley. Mum answered that the only political speech made there was hers, and that everything else should be interpreted as entertainment.

On board the plane, Mum did an airborne walkabout – down the aisle to chat to the travelling press who, like us, were busy consuming champagne in the end-of-term atmosphere.

Ken Parish, who is usually a press attaché for the European Democratic Group, and who had been with us for the whole campaign as a press aide, provided the floorshow. In a pinafore borrowed from one of the air stewardesses, and with a jaunty hat acquired from a passenger, he took charge of the bar service with a flourishing style of filling glasses.

British Island Airways doubles as Air Florida so, in the front cabin, we turned the sign over to Air Florida, and the following announcement was given out over the public address system: 'Ladies and Gentlemen, we are about to land in Miami where it is 5.00 p.m. local time, and the temperature is 32 degrees Centigrade. We hope you enjoyed your flight.'

This raised a cheer from sunlovers, others whose work schedule necessitated their carrying dollars, and some – in the front section of the plane – who were hallucinating about a holiday.

But there is a precedent for high jinks on last flights. In 1979 our final rally took place in Manchester. When we landed at Gatwick after the return flight, the pilot announced that Denis Thatcher had been at the controls for part of the flight.

'Why are we at Luton, then?' yelled a wit in the press end of the aircraft.

The real 'We are about to land . . . etc' announcement came too soon for most of us, including Mum, who was thoroughly enjoying party-time aloft. The last major speech and election television performance were over, the tension of polling day and the count not yet immediate enough to worry about.

As she went forward to sit down for the landing, Mum said, 'What a pity we can't go round again.' She was referring to the airport stacking system, not the campaign trail. Morale on the Prime Ministerial bandwagon was high.

With some opinion polls disagreeing about whether Labour or

124

the Alliance are in second place, I talked to Keith Britto, a mine of information on the polls. Keith is Chris Lawson's deputy director in the marketing department at Conservative Central Office, and one of his tasks during this election campaign has been to commission private opinion polls, and to monitor the others.

The idea of opinion polls was imported to this country from America for the 1945 election, though the technique of taking polls goes back to the last century. The normal sample taken is one thousand people, based on the structure of the population – ie, seeking a representative sample of sex, class and age. During this current campaign over fifty polls have been published, while all the three main parties have been conducting their own private polls. Odd information has leaked out from these, causing a lot of debate: 'We've got David Steel basically saying that their private polls are showing XYZ, which is in conflict with the published polls. Some of the results that we have fed into the computer have also been heavily out of line with everybody else.'

Daily Star, 9 June

" Good morning, sir. I understand you're still undecided "

London Express Service/Daily Star

The new factor in this election is that telephone polls have been used for the first time. This, according to Keith, brings with it new problems, as only about 72 per cent of the electorate have telephones, so that the margin of error in telephone polls is much larger than in face-to-face interviews – where the margin tends to be about three per cent.

I then pointed out to Keith that a lot of people had drawn an analogy between this election, when the Conservatives from the word go have had a big lead, and the 1970 election, when the polls gave Harold Wilson a lead at the end of 18 to 20 per cent, and yet he lost. I asked him whether there was any chance that this could happen again, or had the polls become more sophisticated and accurate?

No, 1970 was an odder situation, when you had a lot of fluctuations, especially towards the end of the campaign. What we've had in this election is almost no change in the Conservative poll throughout the campaign. If you actually look at the trend of the Conservative lead over Labour, it has only fluctuated once. Largely, it has been almost a totally straight line. Our support has remained at around the 45 per cent mark almost solidly. Now, that is totally and utterly unprecedented in any election campaign in which you have had opinion polls in this country. We have had some movements, but they have been within the second and third parties. All the debate yesterday on opinion polls was who is second and who is third.

I asked Keith to try to explain why the Conservative lead has never shrunk or faltered since 9 May, when Mum called the election: 'My personal view is that the electorate had actually made up their minds before the campaign started, and they just haven't changed it. But we have been so successful in the sense of getting over our arguments, there literally has been no scope for movement at all.'

We then discussed the disadvantages and dangers of opinion polls. They can act as accelerating factors in election campaigns, and the French were so concerned about this that they banned them. The problem is to define what is an opinion poll. Party canvassing could be thus described, while private polls cannot be easily banned, and then they get leaked.

Lastly we looked at the political opinion pollsters themselves. I wanted to know how big an industry they were, and how many people and how much money were involved. Keith pointed out that one cannot differentiate, because there is no company that concentrates exclusively on political polling.

> For example, people think of Gallup in political polling terms, but in fact it does a whole range of other work, including Top of the Pops and the charts. They have just developed a new interesting way of doing the charts, involving special recording devices in each record shop and automatic phone-in systems. So, political polling probably only accounts for between 5 and 10 per cent of their turnover.

So we ended, with the unlikely connection between Number One in the hit parade and Number Ten Downing Street.

Wednesday, 8 June

Today was a kind of bonus day – the sun and the sea featured, and there was the added excitement of rides in helicopters, a trendy new observation aircraft (me only), and a hovercraft.

With polling day the next day, there was still some electioneering to do. In our sights today were two seats where we were trying to ward off a considerable Liberal threat, Salisbury in Wiltshire and the Isle of Wight.

The day got off to an unserious start with the eve-of-poll press conference at Conservative Central Office. This bore more resemblance to a script entitled 'Not an Election News Conference' than a serious last word on the issues which would affect the way the electorate voted the next day.

Behind a line of Tory blue-topped miniature bottles of English mineral water (at Mum's insistence, offers of the fizzy French stuff receive a Prime Ministerial scowl), Mum talked with confidence and assurance about securing a mandate for a second term.

Then it was time for open questions, which is apparently press-conferencese for anything goes.

The first questioner, who hailed from Colombia, was greeted with laughter from fellow hacks for a question about Anglo-Latin American relations. A second, this time from Mexico, got similar treatment for prolonging the questioning on relations with that particular part of the universe.

Then followed a German questioner. All these 'foreign funnies' prompted Sir Robin Day to announce himself as a journalist from North Kensington.

He qualified for ultra-courteous treatment from the Prime Minister, who was 'so anxious to make up' for having demoted him to Mr Day throughout her earlier interview on 'Panorama', and was thus happy to let him have a supplementary today.

Party Chairman, Cecil Parkinson, was quick to defend the profession of chartered accountants, of which he is a member, when someone asked whether the number of this species – were there to be a Tory landslide – might constitute a threat to the House of Commons.

That over, we took off from Battersea Heliport for Wiltshire. Three helicopters, ferrying the press, had already departed and we were surprised to learn from ground staff at the Heliport that several of their passengers, who usually spend much time shinning precariously up almost anything which will provide an aerial vantage-point, looked very nervous at being raised aloft officially, powered by two 600-shaft horse-power engines.

Our first drop in was at Old Sarum Airfield, where we were scheduled to tour Edgley Aircraft and see a demonstration flight of the new 'Optica' aircraft.

Mum declined the offer of going up, but I agreed to take her place. Strapped into the no-fuss cabin of this glass-bubble-fronted, buzz-box-type machine, we bumped off along the grass runway like a speeding golf buggy. It was an excellent joyride, although I wasn't sure when pilot, Hugh Field, suggested we see if we could do a bow like a Harrier. Looking at my watch, and consulting the programme, I realized that we were scheduled to leave in about seven minutes and delaying factors like crashes and rescues would undoubtedly prove unpopular.

I got out to hear that Dad had said it was a good thing that brother Mark hadn't been there, because he would have wanted to buy one. The company had no prospect of an order from me, I'm saving up to buy a new car.

Then followed an electioneering half hour when Mum, supporting the Tory Candidate, Robert Key, addressed an open air meeting in the Guildhall Square in Salisbury and roared at demonstrators: 'You're only shouting because you haven't got any arguments left.' The sun shone, which pleased us, and the press, on the orders of the local police at the request of the locals, had been kept off the war memorial, which in turn pleased the locals. Ironically Old Sarum had been one of the great rotten boroughs of the nineteenth century.

The visit wouldn't have been complete without a glimpse at some high tech', and this took the form of a look at UK Provident House's computer system, which stores details of the holders and their insurance policies. Mum absorbed the data while Dad was engrossed in discussing some more tangible statistics – square footage of the office.

Our flight across to the Isle of Wight was blissful. When earlier in the campaign, a thirty-five-minute time-span like this would have been utilized to amend a speech, absorb a briefing, or catch up on signing correspondence, now it was a chance to turn off for half an hour. Those with window seats looked down on the sunny image of England's green and pleasant land, while the helicopter chased its shadow across fields, down dales and over the sparkling Solent.

We landed against the backdrop of the largest Union Jack in the world, covering the hangar doors of the British Hovercraft Corporation in Cowes.

From one form of modern transport, we embarked on another and walked aboard a hovercraft for a nominal hundred-yard trip down to look at its military counterpart. Our advance ashore had journalists searching for the appropriate metaphor to describe Mum rising out of the water, waving through the front window: an entrance which, seen from the shore, would have been a credit to an Andrew Lloyd Webber production or a cinerama film.

Frank Johnson of *The Times* wanted a goddess with whom to compare Maggie. An exotic one, or 'better than Venus', said Alison Ward, who was self appointed mythology researcher for this.

The photographers had an end-of-'Thatcher Tours' stunt up their sleeve, or more accurately, across their chests, in the shape of navy t-shirts bearing the slogan 'Hilda's Personal Photographer'. A worthy journalistic feat this: the research to find Mum's middle name had been done in *Who's Who* and the t-shirt printing executed with hyper-efficient speed.

All the t-shirted media mob lined up in front of the Union Jack, photographed Mum and photographed one another with her, to everyone's amusement.

Mum then spoke to an open air meeting in support of the Tory candidate, Virginia Bottomley. Dad met the Militant Tendency and Mum came as close as she is likely, to wearing a t-shirt when she held up one supporting Virginia against herself.

Time to go, and our helicopter lifted off in a carnival atmosphere. Farewelling wavers found their trouser legs inflating like balloons, their ties straining at the necks as they were blown over their shoulders, and their hairdos and toupees threatened by the hurricane force rotor wash. . . .

The laid back informality of the afternoon had been symbolized by an impromptu saxophone rendition of the National Anthem from a dinghy. Who says that electioneering is all serious?

Half an hour later, and we put down on another water-side landing site – Battersea – and it was back to the real world of the election campaign, as car radios on the way to Number Ten reminded us that the polling stations would be open in about fourteen hours.

POLLING DAY
AND THE COUNT

Thursday, 9 June
Downstairs in the political office at Number Ten, Alison and Tessa were wishing telephone callers 'Happy Polling Day', which was far from the state of affairs upstairs in our flat at 7.05 a.m.

The problem was not anything major like winning or losing the election – in which forty-two million people would be casting their votes in the polling booths which had just opened – but a search for a lost gâteau. The day before, a quite enormous cake of the 'too beautiful to cut' variety – immaculately decorated with blue icing and emblazoned with the Garter *Honi Soit qui Mal y Pense* crest, and 'Victory Again' – had arrived as a good luck present from a London patisserie. Mum wanted to take it up to her constituency to share it with party workers at a polling day lunch which she was hosting.

There was no point looking in the kitchen, which is far too small for such giant examples of gastronomy as sixteen-inch-diameter Grand-Marnier-soaked sponge. Finally it was located down in the cold store and retrieved, defusing the first panic of this long and, at times, rather fraught day.

Mum and Dad went off to vote; they are registered in Westminster, whereas Mark and I had to vote in Chelsea. Mum had wisely decided to get voting out of the way as early as possible in the day.

They were back in the flat by about 7.30 a.m. and Mum sat down to what must have been her first – at any rate cooked – breakfast of the campaign; poached egg on toast.

131

Before she and Dad left to go up to Finchley to tour the committee rooms, I asked her a few things about the campaign, now that it was over and the results lay very much in the hands of Fate.

> **Carol:** What are *your* feelings at this stage in the campaign?
>
> **Margaret Thatcher:** We've worked extremely hard all the time – I think that must help. It is always possible that the polls are wrong. It happened in 1970, and there was a last-minute change in 1974 which the polls didn't detect. But I'm encouraged that the polls have been steady, and I think that means that we shall almost certainly win. I shall be very surprised if we don't. Nevertheless, as you heard me say a few moments ago: 'Now look, we might have to move out of here later today and, if we do, we must be ready.'
>
> **Carol:** Are you nervous?
>
> **Margaret Thatcher:** No, I'm not nervous. I'll just take whatever comes now. We've done our best and a bit more.
>
> **Carol:** You've been out in front in this race, according to newspapers, and according to almost everyone from the word go. Has that in any way made it an easier campaign for you?
>
> **Margaret Thatcher:** No, it hasn't, because I always was prepared for a substantial move in the polls, and I thought that there would be more movement possibly than there has been. Last time we had the same scare campaign, and it did temporarily cause a movement in the polls in the middle of the campaign, which was very unnerving. So, I was prepared for something similar this time, but we did in fact warn people that we should get a scare campaign, and this made it that little bit easier to fight it. But when you start with a big lead it looks simply dreadful if you lose it, because it looks as if it's the way you fought the campaign or something like that. It just means that there's more to live up to.
>
> **Carol:** And you have to be *more* wary of banana skins, in a way.

Margaret Thatcher: That's right.

Carol: What are the events and issues that stick in your mind after this three-week campaign?

Margaret Thatcher: Defence, jobs as part of the economy, putting the facts on our record on the welfare state and home ownership. Home ownership is tremendously important and people in council estates have had the opportunity to buy for the first time.

Carol: Has it bothered you that the campaign, from your point of view, has been conducted either in a media scrum, or with hecklers and demonstrators in quite a lot of places. Is that a strain?

Margaret Thatcher: Hecklers and demonstrators help. They make a campaign much, much more lively. So we're always pleased when we get hecklers and demonstrators. Not just colossal shouting, but so long as you have a loudspeaker that can get over it, it's all right. Your own people then love it – they have something to cheer against and to cheer for.

Carol: What, as Britain's first woman Prime Minister, have you brought to the job?

Margaret Thatcher: I'm not the person to answer that question.

Carol: O.K. How's it changed you?

Margaret Thatcher: I'm not the person to answer that question either. But as I've got to know the job, I have become more and more a square peg in a square hole. As far as I'm concerned, it seems to me that the job and me fit together rather well.

Carol: How, after four years, when all your predecessors have looked positively knackered and exhausted can you look younger and prettier when you go on television?

Margaret Thatcher: Because the job suits me. I've always been used to working hard – as you know – desperately hard. We always had to. But quite apart from that, I like it and it does suit me, and I like doing the work more than almost anything else.

Carol: Do you think the job of Prime Minister is one that actually needs two terms to get into? Do you look on this one as a running-in period?

Margaret Thatcher: No, I wouldn't say a running-in period because many, many people only have one term. I do think that the cumulative experience of one period is immensely valuable to you in a second term, particularly on the international scene. Also, again, you've been through many parliamentary traumas and you know how to cope with those. Indeed, at the end of one term, you've still got a tremendous number of ideas as to what you'd like to do with your second term. And you have a much more accurate assessment of how many of those ideas you're likely to be able to get through, and how many to start on their way with a view to getting them through eventually.

Carol: Do you ever find the limitations and restrictions on normal things you can do too much to bear?

Margaret Thatcher: Not too much to bear. No, one just has to get used to it. You know that if I go shopping, it's not a quiet operation.

Carol: No, that's for sure. Do you think that if you win the election with a landslide or a big majority you can actually claim that you're the new style of Conservatism, appealing to a whole slice of the electorate who'd never have thought of voting Conservative before?

Margaret Thatcher: Conservatism has been in power for a very long time in the general post-war period. We were getting rid of the class idea altogether in British politics during Harold Macmillan's time, and that was when I first stood for Parliament. I always thought that we could get rid of it through home ownership. I think it was Labour who brought back the whole idea in 1964 with their very very class-ridden policies, and I hope *now* that we can get rid of it again, totally, for ever.

Carol: But haven't you been struck, just going round the country this time, by the warmth and strength of support that you've had from a totally different range of people?

Margaret Thatcher: As I say, in this campaign more than any other, we've stressed that in our Party we come from all walks of life, which we do. But that is traditional Conservatism, and it's the Labour Party who has always tried to bring class back into it. Conservatism is an attitude of mind towards the politics of the country, the problems of the country and our role in trying to solve those problems.

Carol: A lot of previous Prime Ministers are quite happy just to stand up and read out a speech which has been presented to them by a speech-writer. You have a very different speech-making philosophy, don't you? It's very much your speech.

Margaret Thatcher: Oh yes, it's got to be my ideas. Not every bit of the draft is mine but, as you know, I go through it all. First we do the ideas, then they go away and draft, then that draft's usually torn up, then we do another one, and then I literally spend hours and hours going through that. We change it and change it, and some speeches we'd still be changing now, if we hadn't delivered them already.

Carol: Are there a lot of hurdles in making a really successful speech, in terms of it reading well, the performance, the audience and the hall?

Margaret Thatcher: Yes, there are. Then, often when you get there you feel you'd like to start all over again. Actually, if it weren't for television and the necessity of press releases, you would make much better speeches, because you'd make your own notes and go and deliver the speech. I do many like that, and those are the best ones really.

Carol: So you think your speech at Fleetwood, when you spoke from your notes, was probably better than one or two of the others?

Margaret Thatcher: No, the ones that I sometimes do on the hustings, and the ones when I am called upon to speak, as at Racal when I opened their new place, because then I have to depend totally on my ideas. There's often quite a clear structure to those speeches, when I think up three points quickly and stick to those.

Carol: Which do you think have been the most influential forms of communication in this election: television speeches, your own walkabouts?

Margaret Thatcher: They're complementary – you've got to do speeches and rallies. Television, I think, is the

135

most powerful form of communication that there is, and herein lies its own dangers, because you often don't get into a thing sufficiently deeply. There are many issues we haven't really gone into in this campaign in any depth.

Carol: Like which?

Margaret Thatcher: We haven't done any environment, although we've spent quite a lot of time considering what we should put in our Manifesto. We haven't done the varying philosophies of the two parties on government. Energy has not come into the campaign in any great way.

Carol: When you called this election, did you think that it was going to be a different campaign to the one which in fact it has turned out to be?

Margaret Thatcher: I think it's different fighting it as a Prime Minister, from what it was as a Leader of the Opposition.

Carol: How would you make the comparison?

Margaret Thatcher: First, as far as press conferences and radio and television appearances are concerned, I've had four years of answering questions in the House, twice a week. The knowledge gained is cumulative and therefore I'm not easily stumped by obscure questions, because the chances are that someone in the House has already asked them.

Carol: So it's been very good training for getting back on the campaign? But a number of your predecessors in Number Ten have actually found, after a spell as Prime Minister in the corridors of power, that it's been quite hard to get back and to adapt to the hustings. You don't appear to have found that at all.

Margaret Thatcher: No, not in any way. No difficulty.

Carol: A lot of people say it's been a hell of a job and a hell of a four years. Why on earth do you want another four years?

Margaret Thatcher: Because it's the job I most want to do in the world and I think I've got something still to give to it.

Carol: You've been a record-breaker already: you're the first scientific Prime Minister, the first woman Prime Minister, and you brought the Callaghan Government

down in fairly historical circumstances. This time, you'll
be the first Conservative Prime Minister since Lord
Salisbury to win a second consecutive term. What does
being a record-breaker mean to you? Is it important?
Margaret Thatcher: The importance lies not in breaking records, but in doing the job when one gets more than
one term. And I think you particularly notice it when
you're dealing with statesmen in other countries. You see
Helmut Schmidt was there for quite a long time; Giscard
was there for seven years – which I don't think is long
enough; but a lot of the people you're dealing with on the
other side of the world are there for twenty years.
Gromyko has been the Soviet Foreign Secretary ever
since I've been in politics. Therefore, I think that from
the viewpoint of dealing with potential adversaries or of
being involved on the international scene, the cumulative
experience is very important. Mrs Gandhi too has been
there a long time, and I think it helps in the forum of a
Commonwealth Conference or of an Economic Summit if
you've been there for quite a time. You must have some
sheet anchors in world democratic politics, because there
are quite a lot in world communist politics with their
totally controlled systems.
Carol: If you win today, have you any other ambitions?
Margaret Thatcher: Well, this is the zenith of my
ambitions.
Carol: It's about 8.20 a.m. now. This time tomorrow
morning, what do you hope the result will be?
Margaret Thatcher: We may not know, because I think
most of the seats will be counted, but there are about
eighty that are not counted till tomorrow morning. A
number of those are redistributed. So, we still may not
know. Obviously I hope to be substantially ahead. Last
time you remember, the count was not started till 9.00
p.m. We didn't know the overall result until about 2.15 in
the afternoon. We've got to go over the halfway number
to be certain.
Carol: You've been fighting elections for thirty years and
have a very good gut reaction about results. What does it
tell you about this one?

Margaret Thatcher: Well, I shall be surprised if we lose. But I don't say that because of the polls. I say that because of the immense response we've had as we've gone round. Also, because of the extreme nature of the Labour Manifesto, it's just not right for this country. I think people prefer the firm style of Government we've had, and the determination to go in a particular direction. I think they know it's right, that the direction we're going in is right, and again their gut feeling is that it's right to continue.

Carol: Are you proud of your first four years?

Margaret Thatcher: I could wish that we hadn't embarked on those first four years at the beginning of a world recession – that wasn't our fault and we weren't to know it. It would have been a tremendous lot easier to do the changes we had to make had we not had a recession. But the actual existence of a world recession made it even more important to do them, otherwise we would have had very little chance of coming out with much hope for Britain.

Carol: Good luck. I must let you go. You look fantastic. See you later.

It hadn't exactly been a formal interview; I was barefoot, and she spent the time swapping the contents of one handbag into another.

I said cheerio, and they set off for Finchley, but not until we'd located Mum's cheque book – she needed it to pay for the lunch.

Number Ten was practically deserted that morning – a sort of cancelled day around the building as everyone waited to find out whether they would have a new boss tomorrow. Sprinting down the corridor which leads from the Cabinet Room to the front door, to leave an envelope of copy of this diary for collection by a messenger, I was struck by the total absence of people around.

At about 3.00 p.m., Mum and Dad reappeared, after touring some thirteen committee rooms and hosting the lunch for party workers at her Conservative Party headquarters in Ballards Lane. Mum retired to bed for a brief rest so that she would be bright and breezy right through the night until five o'clock the following morning, whatever thrills or shocks might be in store in the results. Dad decided to get his head down too. 'We're both bloody bushed' he said. But, before he did, he chatted about his view of the election campaign.

Had he enjoyed being campaign co-star, I enquired? He hadn't been a campaign co-star, he thought, and he saw attempts by the press to make him out to be a second Duke of Edinburgh as a 'total absurdity'.

'I've done the job for a good long time. I've been six foot behind, trying not to make any mistakes, doing as much good as I can', is how he chose to phrase the job description of being the Prime Minister's consort.

Turning his mind to the election results, he said that he was sure that we were going to win, but hoped that we would secure the magic number of seats – 326 – under our belts before we went to bed the following morning.

He rated the election as an historic one, because the SDP, when it was formed, had talked about breaking the mould of politics in Britain. Now it looked as though it was the Prime Minister who would be doing just that.

I woke Mum with a cup of tea shortly before 5.00 p.m., before I went off to Chelsea Town Hall to vote. Leaving Number Ten swinging my ignition keys, I discovered that my car had been towed away to I knew not where, because the space was needed for the television crews. I amended my travelling plans and walked to the Tube station instead.

Walking down the King's Road from Sloane Square provided a brief intermission in the real world during my campaign-dominated existence.

Back at Number Ten, I found that Beating Retreat was in full musical progress on Horse Guards, while in Downing Street the media circus was setting up for the night's interminable election coverage. Camera crews were moving into position, and linking up with their giant outside broadcast vans, parked down the steps which lead to St James's Park. This is the first election to be held since the birth of breakfast television, which will presumably carry on when the traditional election coverage leaves off at dawn.

ITN had also scored a first with the incorporation in the

Prime Minister's car of a portable television camera focused on Mum's seat. Their plan was to film her as she left Hendon Town Hall after the count, arrived at Ballards Lane, and left again for Conservative Central Office in Smith Square. It is an ingenious piece of new technology, and an exclusive innovation for ITN. But there was little high tech' in the method whereby the Prime Minister could stop herself being filmed if she so wished. She could simply put a black cloth over the camera lens!

I raced up to the flat, which was filling up with beautiful flowers and was heady with their scent. Good luck cakes, including one with a larger-than-life-sized face of Mum iced on its top, were also pouring in.

Mum was downstairs, being interviewed and having her photograph taken for *Time* Magazine, on whose cover she is to appear next week. I had my hair done, while the hairdresser waited for her to come up for a wash and set.

Mum opted to wear a simple navy dress, which she'd worn for several rallies during the campaign. I had put out a more glamorous blue number – one of her favourites – but she rejected it with the tactful and thoughtful reasoning which is her through and through.

'No, it's too much. Some people are going to lose tonight.'

Mark had returned from America, and was around to lend support, while Dad was closeted in his study, finishing off correspondence. This was to be the first night for weeks that there hadn't been a speech-writing session, and Crawfie was preparing a cold supper so that the family could have a civilized bite to eat in peace and quiet. We all sat down for a drink, basically very confident but with that slight sense of unease which comes as the results approach. Cecil Parkinson arrived for supper. For both the Chairman and the Leader of the Party, these hours of waiting must have been agonizing but they disguised their up-tightness stoically. We consumed roast lamb and salad, strawberries and cream at Mum's fast-eating pace. She then talked to Cecil in the sitting room until it was time for him to go to his Hertfordshire constituency, Hertsmere. The rest of us, meanwhile, watched the television, waiting for the first straw poll results.

At eleven o'clock, it was time for us to leave Number Ten to go up to Finchley for the count. The front hall of the house looked like a stage set, illuminated by the brilliant television lights just outside the windows. As we stood waiting for the sign that Mum's car was ready, we talked to Peter Taylor, Number Ten's house manager, and the messengers. Mum was quite tense, but Dad joked his way through.

As she stepped out into the brilliant lights in the street, Mum was asked by a television interviewer whether she considered herself home and dry in the election, as the television polls were already forecasting a Conservative majority of 116 seats. She smartly riposted, 'I consider that this will be my home for the next five years.' With that, she was off and away to Finchley.

At Hendon Town Hall we were all ushered into a rather stark room, to sit and wait to see whether the results would prove as good as we hoped. Mum, Dad, Mark, Derek Howe,

The Sun, 9 June

"THERE'S A COUPLE OF CROSSES MARKED FOR YOU ALREADY"

London Express Service/The Sun

Joy Robilliard, Roger Boaden and David Boddy began to watch the television, while Andrew Thomson, Mum's agent in Finchley, popped in and out with news of how the count was going on the other side of the passage. Of the eleven opponents challenging Mum in Finchley, one had already fallen by the wayside. Colin Hanoman lost his appeal in the High Court last week to change his name by deed poll to Margaret Thatcher.* He is now facing a bill of £6,000 for costs – a very stiff amount compared to the mere £150 deposit taken out by the other candidates.

This deposit was fixed in 1918, when £150 was a large amount of money. With inflation, its deterrent effect has decreased sharply – hence a proposal from a Commons select committee to raise the deposit to £1,000, and another from Conservative agents that candidates should require fifty signatures rather than the present ten for their names to go forward.

The comparative smallness of the deposit has meant that Mum had some very eccentric opponents. Apart from the Labour and Liberal Alliance candidates, they ranged from Helen Mary Anscomb – whose surname ensured that she was the first to have her count registered – standing for Independent: Rail not Motorway, to Benjamin Collingham Wedmore who, standing for Belgrano Bloodhunger, recalled the unpleasant connotations of Denis Healey's attack on Mum earlier in the campaign.

Simone Wilkinson is one of the Greenham Peace Women, campaigning as a Women-Life on Earth and Ecology Party candidate – one of her colleagues was standing against Michael Heseltine in his Henley constituency. An ex-Coronation Street actor, David Alec Webb, was riding on the Anti-Censorship, Reform of the Obscene Publications Act ticket, while the licensing lobby found Anthony Joseph Noonan, Ban Every Licensing Law Society, and Brian Clifford Wareham, Party of Association with Licensees. That familiar campaigning figure, Lord David Edward Sutch, fresh from defeat at Bermondsey, represented the Official Monster Raving Loony Party, with a manifesto to bring back the village idiot and replace road tax with petrol tax. The fringe

* I am grateful to Iris Peters of the *Hendon Times* for information on the candidates.

was completed by Anthony Peter Whitehead, dressed in Batman costume, and campaigning for law and order in Gotham City. His aim was to secure posperity by entering the *Guinness Book of Records* for polling the smallest ever number of votes.

In the last election in 1979, Mum held the seat with a poll of 20,918, and a majority of nearly 8,000 over the Labour candidate, with the Liberal third, and the National Front and an Independent Democrat bringing up the rear.

This time, her Labour opponent was Laurence Spigel, a thirty-year-old social worker for Camden Council. A left-winger, he is a supporter of CND and a borough councillor in Barnet. According to all reports, he had been maintaining an energetic campaign, and was believed to have drawn ahead of the Alliance candidate, Dr Margaret Jane Joachim. She is thirty-three, a computer consultant, and shares with Mum a scientific training at Oxford. She claimed that her latest canvass returns would give her 40 per cent of the vote, but this, like the national opinion polls, was disputed by the other candidates.

Mum's agent in Finchley, Andrew Thomson, had been working with her for the past fifteen months. He has had, in a way, a harder task than most agents, because his prospective parliamentary candidate was also the Leader of the Conservative Party and Prime Minister. As such, she had spent rather less time in her constituency than most candidates. As you have seen in this diary, she has visited Finchley on five occasions during the campaign: for her adoption meeting, on two of the Saturdays, on the eve of poll, and now, of course, on polling day.

Andrew was in no doubt that Mum would romp home in the count, and he was looking for her to increase the 52 per cent of the vote that she won in 1979.

ITN meanwhile was prattling away with its racetrack to Westminster forecasts, its swings, exit polls, and fancy graphics. Its first forecast was a comfortable majority of 116, but the early results were showing an ominous swing to the Liberals.

Ten past midnight, and we lost Yeovil to the Liberals. 'This is very bad,' Mum reacted, looking dark, hand across brow, scribbling notes.

It wasn't until we gained Nuneaton from Labour at 12.16 – a result that produced much clapping and cheering – that things started to look a little brighter.

Once the Conservative gains started coming in thick and fast, our tense expressions turned to smiles and exclamations of delight. Mum was particularly delighted when David Evennett won the Kent constituency of Erith and Crayford for the Tories. She had fought down there unsuccessfully as the Conservative candidate in the 1950 and 1951 elections, and had got engaged to Dad during the second campaign, so this success was special for her.

Our chief problem was that the count in Finchley was progressing at a snail's pace – very frustrating.

Disappointment followed with the Isle of Wight result. Virginia Bottomley, whom we had been down to support the previous day, failed to conquer the Liberals.

2.20 a.m.: ITN flashed up a note to the effect that the Conservatives needed only fifteen more seats for the magic winning total of 326. Mum said drily, 'Ours is one, I trust.'

She watched Michael Foot concede defeat in silence. She was totally absorbed with the responsibility of winning, rather than with celebrating victory.

Briefly, she hoped that the 326th seat might be hers, but it wasn't. We cheered and clapped when it came up. 'Mrs Thatcher is back in Number Ten Downing Street,' Alastair Burnet announced. He was corrected by the lady herself, getting rapidly more exasperated by the fact that the declaration of her results had been expected over an hour earlier. 'No, I'm still at Hendon Town Hall,' she retorted in response to Alastair Burnet.

Eventually the returning officer was ready. In a chamber full of supporters of some of the eccentric fringe candidates, we waited for the declaration. With a count of 19,616, Mum's majority over the Labour candidate, Laurence Spigel, was 9,314, 1,436 up on the 1979 result. Anthony Whitehead had not achieved his aim of securing entry into the *Guinness Book of Records*: his poll of 37 was an improvement on Brian Wareham, 27, David Webb, 28, and bringing up the rear, Benjamin Wedmore and his Belgrano Bloodhunger, 13.

Mum couldn't have looked less like a triumphant Prime Minister who had just won an historic victory and was heading for a substantial majority in the new House of Commons. She looked and sounded tense.

As she stood to move the vote of thanks of behalf of her fellow candidates, one – Mr Webb of the Anti-Censorship lobby – waved an umbrella with his message printed in large letters.

The scene was definitely rather a shambolic one. The motorized winding-on of film, and massed clicking from the photographers in the public gallery every time she turned their way, almost drowned her words and provoked laughter from the audience. Many of them looked as though they would be more at home at a fancy dress party than a count, such was the mode of attire worn by some of the supporters of the more bizarre candidates. Lord Sutch of the Official Monster Raving Loony Party was himself wearing lurex, leopard-spotted trousers and a red top hat.

Mum made a very low-key vote of thanks on behalf of her fellow candidates, interrupted briefly by the Anti-Censorship candidate. She expressed her pride and honour in representing Finchley and Friern Barnet once again. 'It has been a rather exciting evening for some of us and I have reason to think that we may have been returned to serve nationally for another period in Government.' It was far from a victorious speech. You could read relief and satisfaction between the lines, but it contained no euphoric rhetoric. She went on to say that she approached that second term of office with a very great sense of responsibility and humility, and ended by saying: 'I just want to thank my husband Denis', which met with applause. The man standing next to me remarked, 'Will she make Kenny Everett her Foreign Secretary?'

It appeared that some people that night had found counts less stodgy and more entertaining than they had anticipated. On the way out of Hendon Town Hall, the man in front of me concluded, 'What with this, and Jasper Carrott, it hasn't been a bad evening'. Because she was running very late, Mum left almost immediately to go to thank her own party workers. Her next port of call was Conservative Central Office, to thank staff there before the television went off.

Television lights and a small crowd greeted us outside in Smith Square, on what was dawning as a beautiful day. Inside, staff lined the stairs and the landings, waiting to welcome and congratulate Mum. Rapturous applause surrounded her as she walked up to the first floor with Dad and Mark.

In a short speech, she said: 'Power is a trust and we must exercise it in that way.'

It was rather a tired party by the time we arrived – well after 4.00 a.m. Most of the people had spent a hard day canvassing and working in constituencies, and many had had an exhausting three-week campaign. There was a dazed but happy expression on their faces.

Mum with Dad and Cecil Parkinson, waved happily from a first-floor window. Dad made a point of going round to thank all the behind-the-scenes workers whom Mum wouldn't get around to seeing that night.

Mum, sitting at a table in a conference room – a venue more suited to crisis talks than to a champagne celebration – relaxed joked, laughed and began to enjoy her spectacular triumph at the polls. With her were the Parkinsons, their three daughters, Sir Geoffrey and Lady Howe, Ian and Jane Gow and several others, who had returned from their constituencies.

I got back ahead of them to Number Ten with photographer Herbie Knott to take returning-to-Number-Ten photographs. It was lining up to be a beautiful day and there was an excited air of expectancy from both the crowd gathered on the corner of Whitehall, and the media mob massed behind a crash barrier at the St James's Park end of Downing Street.

As well as the television lights outside, we now had them in the hall too. Television executives obviously had the same idea in mind for their screens as I had for this diary – a shot of Mum coming in through the front door – a famous entry across a famous threshold. Herbie was in position in the hall, while I got ready to lean out of a first-floor window to take the aerial shot of the arrival.

This was a complicated arrangement because I then had to belt back down the stairs at a dangerous speed to return the lens to Herbie for his photograph. We gambled on the fact that Mum would wave outside for longer than it would take me to get down inside.

The convoy at last turned into Downing street and as soon as
Mum emerged from her car she went over to the television
cameras and photographers, before beetling off down to the
Whitehall end of the street. She had done the same on the night
that the Falklands conflict ended, in order to thank supporters.
Downing Street, these days, is usually closed to the public for
security reasons, but she hates not being able to thank people
who have waited a long time to see her and have given her such
a rousing welcome.

Mum waved wildly to the world, from the front step of
Number Ten, before she and Dad turned to come inside – an
historic entrance into a house of history.

'Welcome home,' greeted the house manager, Peter Taylor,
shaking her hand. After 'landslide victory', these must have
been the two most heart-warming words she had heard that
night.

'Good evening, good morning,' joked Mum to the small
group of Special Branch, messengers and others in the front
hall. She wasn't sure which of them, like her, were finishing the
marathon of 9 June, and which were merely at the start of a new
day of work. She and Dad went up by lift to the flat, as I ran
along the corridor past the Cabinet Room – which was being
hoovered – and up the main stairs, lined with the portraits of
past Prime Ministers, in whose ranks Mum tonight had earned
herself such a special place.

'Congratulations,' I said, 'I'm thrilled for you.' As she got
ready to go to bed, I carried on, 'It's history.' She thoughtfully
interposed, 'But history, when you're making it, doesn't seem
like history.'

'They expect you to jump up and down but you're always
thinking of the next job in hand.'

'I wonder if there is world news,' she queried, picking up her
bedside transistor radio.

'I think you'll find you're it,' I said.

It was 5.10 a.m.

The Campaign Programme

Programme for Friday, 20 May 1983
VISIT TO WESTERN AREA

08.15	Arrive Central Office
08.30 – 09.25	Prime Minister's Briefing Meeting
09.30 – 10.00	Daily News Conference – Ground Floor Conference Room
10.00 – 10.20	Private discussion between Prime Minister and Chairman
10.20	Provision for Media Interviews
10.45	Depart Central Office by car for Victoria Station
11.00	Train to Gatwick Station – (arrive 11.41) – transfer to car
12.15	Flight take-off from Gatwick (lunch on board) Destination: St Mawgan Flying Time: 1 hour
13.15	Arrive St Mawgan To be met by: Mr Peter Gower, CBE – Central Office Agent Mr Gordon Shattock – Western Area Chairman Join Campaign Coach to leave at 13.30
13.55	Arrive Padstow Harbour (North Cornwall constituency) Visit fish tanks and meet Fishermen/Merchants/ Harbour Master at quayside Walk along quayside and meet supporters
14.35	Depart Padstow
14.50	Arrive Trelyll Farm, near Wadebridge (North Cornwall) Owner Mr W. D. Nightingale – a large dairy farm – meet farmers and families
15.20	Depart Trelyll Farm
15.30	Arrive Molesworth Street car park, Wadebridge to meet supporters from North Cornwall and Truro constituencies
16.00	Depart St Mawgan Destination: Gatwick Airport Flying Time: 1 hour
17.00	Arrive Gatwick – transfer to car for return to London
18.00	Approx. – arrive Number Ten Provision for meeting Robin Butler Provision for speech preparation

Programme for Saturday, 21 May 1983
VISIT TO FINCHLEY

09.15	Depart Number Ten by car for High Road Finchley
10.00	Walkabout from the High Road, visiting: Budgen's Supermarket Chivers Brothers Motors Bryson's the printers and a number of roads
12.00	Approx.: Mrs Thatcher's Campaign Headquarters, 212 Ballards Lane, Finchley, London N12
14.00	Depart Finchley for Number Ten by car

Programme for Monday, 23 May 1983
VISIT TO WESTERN AREA/WALES

08.15	Arrive Central Office
08.30 – **09.25**	Prime Minister's Briefing Meeting
09.30 – **10.00**	Daily News Conference – Ground Floor Conference Room
10.00 – **10.20**	Private discussion between Prime Minister and Chairman
10.20	Provision for Media Interviews
10.45	Depart Central Office by car for Battersea Heliport
11.00	Take off by helicopter Destination: Filton – British Aerospace Flying Time: 50 minutes

11.50	Arrive Filton
	To be met by: Mr Peter Gower, CBE – Central Office Agent
	                   Mr Gordon Shattock – Western Area Chairman
	                   Mr Jack Aspinwall – Candidate for Wansdyke
	                   Mr Michael Wilde – Managing Director British
	                   Aerospace
	Join Campaign Coach

12.15	Arrive Longwell Green Community Centre (Wansdyke Constituency) Meet approximately 150 elderly citizens. Those present will also include: Mr Jack Aspinwall, Conservative Candidate for Wansdyke, Mrs Aspinwall, and candidates from surrounding constituencies
13.15	Lunch with Luncheon Club
13.45	Depart Longwell Green Community Centre
14.00	Arrive premises of Messrs Bristol Erickson Ltd, Tower Road, North Warmley Machine Tool manufacturers Managing Director: Mr M. S. Neal
14.45	Depart Bristol Erickson Ltd by road for Cardiff
16.00	Approx. Arrive Angel Hotel Cardiff To be met by: Mr Zachary Brierley, Wales Area Chairman Mr Ted Thurgood – Central Office Agent
16.30	Provision for Regional Interviews
17.40	Provision for telephone conversation with Chairman
18.00	Dinner in Suite
19.00	Depart Angel Hotel Cardiff
19.04	Arrive City Hall – Committee Room A
19.15	Welsh Area Rally
20.15	Depart City Hall: (a) Prime Minister to return to London by car (b) Rest of tour party to travel to Rhoose Airport
21.00	Flight back to London Gatwick for tour party
21.50	Arrive Gatwick Airport – transfer to coaches
22.45	Arrive Central London

Programme for Tuesday, 24 May 1983
VISIT TO SOUTH-EASTERN AREA

08.15	Arrive Central Office

08.30 – 09.25	Prime Minister's Briefing Meeting
09.30 – 10.00	Daily News Conference – Ground Floor Conference Room
10.00 – 10.20	Private discussion between Prime Minister and Chairman
10.20	Provision for Media Interviews
11.15	Depart Central Office by car for Battersea Heliport
11.30	Take off by Helicopter for Deal
12.00	Arrive Royal Marine Depot, Canada Road, Deal To be met by: Mr & Mrs Peter Rees and others Join Campaign Coach
12.15	Arrive Walmer Lifeboat Station to meet members of the crew and voluntary supporters from the RNLI and the Ladies Lifeboat Guild
12.40	Depart for Deal Conservative Office
12.45	Arrive Deal Conservative Office To be met by: Mr James Thompson – Chairman Deal Conservative Branch Mrs Sally Le Faye – Secretary Deal Conservative Branch
13.00	Depart for Dover
13.30	Arrive Dover Promenade opposite Harbour Board HQ. Meet Harbour Board Officials and view the Harbour Chairman: Sir Frederick Bolton, MC Managing Director & Registrar: Mr W. T. Allen, MBE, BSc, CEng
13.45	Working Lunch with Harbour representatives
14.15	Depart for Dover Party HQ
14.30	Arrive Dover Party HQ To be met by: Mr Fred Cleary, CBE – President Dover Conservative Association Mrs Ruth Purnell – Chairman Dover Conservative Association
15.00	Depart from Connaught Barracks by helicopter for Battersea
15.30	Arrive Battersea Heliport Leave by car for Downing Street
16.00	Approx. – arrive Downing Street Briefing prior to 'Nationwide'
17.15	Depart for BBC Television Studios (Lime Grove)
17.45	Arrive BBC Television Studios
18.25	TV 'Nationwide' programme
19.15	Return to Downing Street

Programme for Wednesday, 25 May 1983
VISIT TO EAST OF ENGLAND AREA

08.15	Arrive Central Office
08.30 – 09.25	Prime Minister's Briefing Meeting
09.30 – 10.00	Daily News Conference – Ground Floor Conference Room
10.00 – 10.20	Private discussion between Prime Minister and Chairman
10.20	Provision for Media Interviews

150

10.45	Depart Central Office by car for Victoria Station
11.00	Train to Gatwick Station
12.00	Flight take-off from Gatwick (lunch on board)
	Destination: RAF Marham, Norfolk
	Flying time: 55 minutes
12.55	Arrive RAF Marham
	To be met by: W. R. Henderson – COA Eastern Area
	Sir Paul Hawkins – PPC South-west Norfolk
	Mr Brian Tooke – East of England Area Chairman
	Join Campaign Coach. Depart for Narborough village
13.05	Arrive Narborough village
	Whistlestop
	Escorted by Sir Paul Hawkins, PPC
	South-west Norfolk
13.15	Depart for Castle Acre village
13.25	Arrive Castle Acre village green
	To be met by: Henry Bellingham – PPC
	North-west Norfolk
	Address rally for North-west Norfolk
	Conservative workers and villagers
13.40	Depart Castle Acre for East Dereham
14.00	Arrive East Dereham Market Square
	To be met by: Richard Ryder – PPC Mid-Norfolk
	Address Mid-Norfolk rally for Conservative workers and general
	public in Dereham Market Place
14.10	Depart East Dereham for Norfolk County Showground, Costessey
14.27	Divert off A47 to Hockering village
14.30	Three-minute stop with Mid-Norfolk supporters and villagers
14.45	Arrive Norfolk County Showground, Costessey Address rally for
	workers and supporters from Norfolk constituencies
	Meet Candidates for Norfolk constituencies
15.10	Depart County Showground for Norwich Airport
15.25	Arrive Norwich Airport – Airport Managers' office
	Press Conference/Interviews: BBC East, Anglia TV,
	local radio stations and newspapers
16.00	Flight back to London Gatwick
16.45	Arrive Gatwick Airport
17.40	Arrive Central London

Programme for Thursday, 26 May 1983
VISIT TO THE YORKSHIRE AREA

08.15	Arrive Central Office
08.30 – **09.25**	Prime Minister's Briefing Meeting
09.30 – **10.00**	Daily News Conference – Ground Floor Conference Room
10.00 – **10.20**	Private discussion between Prime Minister and Chairman
10.20	Provision for Media Interviews
10.45	Depart Central Office by car for Victoria Station
11.00	Train to Gatwick Station

11.45	Flight take-off from Gatwick Destination: Leeds Bradford Airport Flying time: 1 hour
12.45	Arrive Leeds Bradford Airport To be met by: Mr Eric Ward – COA Yorkshire Mr Joe Barnard – Yorkshire Area Chairman
13.00	Join Campaign Coach
13.10	Arrive Harry Ramsden's Restaurant: Lunch General Manager: Mr Frank Begg
13.50	Depart Harry Ramsden's via Menston for Otley
13.55	Whistlestop – Menston (suburban village in Shipley)
14.00	Depart Menston for Otley
14.10	Arrive Otley – Robert Ogden Holdings Tour of premises Robert Ogden Holdings To be escorted by: Mr Robert Ogden, Chairman and Managing Director
14.40	Depart via Huby for Harrogate
14.48	Whistlestop – Huby village centre (Skipton and Ripon) To be met by: Mr John Watson, Candidate
14.53	Depart Huby for Harrogate
15.03	Arrive Police Convalescent Home, Harrogate To be met by: Supt R. J. Webb, QPM Tour of Convalescent Home
15.30	Depart Police Convalescent Home for Majestic Hotel, Harrogate
15.35	Arrive Majestic Hotel, Harrogate General Manager: Mr Frank Flaherty
16.00	Briefing and speech preparation
17.00	Regional interviews: Television, Radio, etc
18.00	Light supper
19.00	Depart Majestic Hotel for Royal Hall, Harrogate
19.05	Arrive Royal Hall, Harrogate
19.15	Harrogate Rally: Chairman Mr Joe Barnard (Yorkshire Area Chairman)
20.30	Depart for Leeds Bradford Airport
21.00	Flight from Leeds Bradford to Gatwick
22.00	Arrive Gatwick – transfer to coaches
22.55	Arrive Central London

Programme for Friday, 27 May 1983
VISIT TO THE WESSEX AREA

08.15	Arrive Central Office
08.30 – 09.25	Prime Minister's Briefing Meeting
09.30 – 10.00	Daily News Conference – Ground Floor Conference Room
10.00 – 10.20	Private discussion between Prime Minister and Chairman
10.20	Provision for Media Interviews
10.45	Depart Central Office by car for Battersea Heliport

11.00	Flight take-off from Battersea Heliport
	Destination: Recreation Ground, Tilehurst, Reading
	Flying Time: 20 minutes
11.20	Arrive Recreation Ground, Tilehurst, Reading
	To be met by: Mr David Roberts – COA Wessex Area
	Mr Hugh Simmonds – Hon. Treasurer Wessex Area
	Join Campaign Coach
11.35	Depart for Tempatron, Reading
	Rendezvous with Press Coaches
11.45	Arrive Tempatron, Portman Road, Reading
	To be joined by: Mr Tony Durant – Candidate Reading West
	Mrs Audrey Durant
	Mr Arthur James – Chairman Reading West
	To be met by: Mr Bill McNab – Managing Director
	and fellow Directors
	Tour factory accompanied by Mr McNab and fellow Directors
12.15	Depart Tempatron for Racal Research Ltd, via Honey End Lane
12.20	Arrive Honey End Lane Shopping Precinct
	Whistlestop – meet Party workers from Reading East and West
12.40	Arrive Racal Research Ltd, Reading
	To be joined by: Dr Gerard Vaughan – Candidate Reading East
	Mrs Thurle Vaughan
	To be met by: Sir Ernest Harrison, OBE – Chairman Racal Group
	Mr Geoffrey Lomer – Director Racal Group
	Directors of companies in the Racal Group
	Tour of new Micro-Electronics Research and
	Development Department
	Official opening of new building
13.10	Lunch in Canteen of Racal Research Ltd
	Luncheon party to include: Mr and Mrs Tony Durant
	Dr and Mrs Gerard Vaughan
	Mr David Roberts – COA Wessex Area
	Mr Hugh Simmonds
	– Hon. Treasurer Wessex
13.50	Depart Racal Research for Racal Mobilcal, Reading
13.55	Arrive Racal Mobilcal, Basingstoke Road, Reading
	To be met by: Sir Ernest Harrison, OBE and fellow Directors
	Dr Gerard Vaughan – Candidate Reading East
	Tour of factory
14.30	Depart Racal Mobilcal for Quantel Ltd, Newbury
	via Thatcham
14.45	Arrive Broadway, Thatcham
	Whistlestop – meet Party workers from Newbury
15.00	Arrive Quantel Ltd, Turnpike Road, Newbury
	To be met by: Mr Peter Michael – Chairman
	Mr Richard Taylor – Managing
	Director and fellow Directors
	Mr Michael McNair-Wilson – Candidate Newbury
	Mrs Deidre McNair-Wilson
	Mrs Aldina Pyne – Chairman
	Newbury Conservative Association
	Tour of factory and demonstration of Paintbox
15.45	Depart Quantel Ltd for Instrumental Colour Systems, Newbury
15.50	Arrive Instrumental Colour Systems, Newbury
	To be met by: Mr Anthony Perry – Chairman
	Mr John Harding – Publicity Manager
	Mrs Polly Perry

	Tour of factory The Prime Minister will unveil a plaque and declare the new building open
16.10	Depart Instrumental Colour Systems for Newbury Race Course
16.15	Arrive Newbury Race Course for take-off to Battersea Heliport
16.35	Approx. – arrive Battersea Heliport
16.55	Arrive Downing Street

Programme for Tuesday, 31 May 1983
VISIT TO SCOTLAND

08.15	Arrive Central Office
08.30 – 09.25	Prime Minister's Briefing Meeting
09.30 – 10.00	Daily News Conference – Ground Floor Conference Room
10.00 – 10.20	Private discussion between Prime Minister and Chairman
10.20	Depart Central Office for Downing Street
10.30	Prepare for and record 'Panorama'
13.00	Lunch in flat
13.45	Depart Number Ten by car for Victoria Station
14.00	Train to Gatwick (arrive 14.41)
15.00	Flight take-off from Gatwick Destination: Edinburgh Airport Flying Time: 80 minutes
16.20	Arrive Edinburgh Turnhouse Airport To be met by: Mr Michael Ancram – Chairman Scottish Conservative Party Mr A. M. G. Macmillan – Director of Scottish Conservative Party
16.25	Depart Edinburgh Airport for Scottish Central Office
16.40	Arrive Scottish Central Office 3 Chester Street, Edinburgh
16.55	Depart Scottish Central Office for Caledonian Hotel, Edinburgh
17.00	Arrive Caledonian Hotel, Edinburgh To be met by: Rt Hon. George Younger – Secretary of State for Scotland
19.00	Depart Caledonian Hotel for George Watson's College
19.12	Arrive George Watson's College To be met by: Mr Adam Currie – The Master, Edinburgh Merchants Co. Dr Roger Young – Headmaster, George Watson's College Mr Donald Maclean – President SCUA
19.15	Scottish Rally Address Rally for ten Lothian Region Constituencies (Six in Edinburgh and four outside) Chairman: Mr Donald Maclean Those present to include: The Secretary of State Candidates for Lothian Region Constituences (one of whom is Michael Ancram)
20.10	Depart George Watson's College for Edinburgh Airport

20.35	Flight take-off from Edinburgh Airport Destination: Inverness Flying Time: 30 minutes
21.05	Arrive Dalcross Airport, Inverness To be met by: David Maclean – Candidate Inverness Nairn and Lochabar Mrs Lorna Waddell – Constituency Chairman Pipers
21.35	Arrive Station Hotel, Inverness (Manager Mr Tom Gilchrist) Supper in Suite Overnight stay, Station Hotel

Programme for Wednesday, 1 June 1983
VISIT TO HIGHLAND & GRAMPIAN
CONSTITUENCIES/NORTH-WEST AREA

08.30	TV Interviews
08.50	Depart Station Hotel
09.00	Arrive Tarka Controls Ltd To be met by: Mr Jeremy Nichols – Managing Director David Maclean – Candidate Inverness Nairn and Lochabar Mrs Lorna Waddell – Constituency Chairman
09.45	Depart Tarka Controls Ltd
10.45	Arrive James Johnston & Co of Elgin Ltd, Cashmere & Woollen Manufacturers, Newmill, Elgin To be met by: Mr John Harrison – Company Chairman Mr Alex Pollock – Candidate Moray Mr Ian McLaren – Constituency Chairman (Sir Russell Sanderson is a Director of Johnstons)
11.30	Meet the Scottish Press, Room at Johnstons of Elgin The travelling press depart on their buses for RAF Lossiemouth
11.40	Depart Elgin
12.00	Depart RAF Lossiemouth Flying Time: 1 hour and 6 minutes
13.06	Arrive Manchester International Airport (Ringway) To be met by: Cllr Ken Franklin – Chairman (Labour) C/Cllr Gordon Thomas – Vice Chairman (Labour) Mr Gil Thompson – Chief Executive Mr Don Brewin – Director of Operations Mr Bill Charnock – Commercial Manager
13.15	Inspect Airport Developments (Developments concerned with turning Manchester into a major international airport)
13.45	Interview at Airport with Granada TV (VVIP Lounge)
14.00	Depart from Airport
14.25	Warburton's Bakery, Back o' th' Bank Bakery, Hereford Street, Bolton Tour of Bakery To be met by: Mr Derrick Warburton Mr Tom Warburton – Joint Chairmen Mr George Warburton Mr Henry Warburton – Directors Mr Jim Speak – Managing Director Mr Alan Hood – Divisional Manager Mr Peter Haworth – General Manager (Bakery)
15.05	Depart

15.10	Arrive Bolton Business Venture, 46 Lower Bridgeman Street, Bolton
	To be met by: Mr Derrick Warburton – Chairman
	Mr Roger McMullan – Director
	Introduced to: Mr D. Buxton – Director of the Chamber of Commerce
	Mr P. Bounds – Chief Executive of the Bolton Metropolitan District Council
15.20	Depart
15.45	Arrive Frederic Robinson Ltd, Unicorn Brewery, Stockport, Cheshire
	Tour of brewery
	To be met by: Mr Peter Robinson – Chairman and Director
	Mr David Robinson
	Mr Dennis Robinson – Directors
16.15	Depart
16.15	Interview (on the coach) with BBC Television, Manchester
	Interviewer: Mr David Davies
16.30	Arrive Manchester International Airport
	Picture story with Conservative Candidates for the Manchester Seats:
	Manchester Blackley – Peter Ridgway
	Manchester Central – Dave Eager
	Manchester Gorton – John Kershaw
	Manchester Withington – Fred Silvester
	Manchester Wythenshawe – Mrs Joan Jacobs

Programme for Thursday, 2 June 1983
VISIT TO THE EAST MIDLANDS AREA

08.15	Arrive Central Office
08.30 – 09.25	Prime Minister's Briefing Meeting
09.30 – 10.00	Daily News Conference – Ground Floor Conference Room
10.00 – 10.20	Private discussion between Prime Minister and Chairman
10.20	Provision for Media Interviews
10.45	Depart Central Office by car for Victoria Station
11.00	Train to Gatwick Station
12.00	Flight take-off from Gatwick (lunch on board)
	Destination: East Midland Airport (Castle Donington)
	Flying Time: 45 minutes
12.45	Arrive East Midlands Airport
	To be met by: Candidates and supporters from Amber Valley, Bosworth, Broxtowe, Derby North and South, Erewash, Gedling, Melton, Loughborough, Nottingham East, North and North and South, Rushcliffe and South Derbyshire
	Join Campaign Coach
13.00	Depart East Midlands Airport for Shepshed, The Bull Ring
13.15	Arrive Shepshed (North-West Leicestershire Constituency)
	Whistlestop
	To be met by: David Ashby – Candidate, North-West Leicestershire and supporters

13.20	Depart Shepshed for Leicester
	As coaches pass through the Bosworth Constituency
	before reaching Leicester, Adam Butler's supporters
	will be at the roadside to let off blue balloons
13.45	Arrive Town Hall Square, Leicester
	To be met by: Candidates for Leicester East, South and West
	West and supporters
	Open air meeting in Town Hall Square, Leicester
	(Note: There will be an RAF Careers Display in the Town Hall
	Square at the same time, featuring a Harrier)
14.05	Depart Town Hall Square for T. W. Kempton Ltd,
	Burley's Way, Leicester
14.10	Arrive T. W. Kempton Ltd
	To be met by: Mr Neville Kempton – Joint Managing Director
	Tour of knitwear factory. Sample to be presented to Prime Minister
14.40	Depart T. W. Kempton Ltd for Market Harborough
15.05	Arrive Market Harborough (Harborough Constituency)
	Whistlestop
	To be met by: John Farr – Candidate, Harborough, and supporters
15.10	Depart Market Harborough for Burton Latimer
15.35	Arrive Burton Latimer to visit Weetabix Ltd
	To be met by: Mr Richard George – Chairman
	and Joint Managing Director
	Mr William George – President
	and Joint Managing Director
	and other senior Directors
	Tour factory – principally new block where Weetabix is produced
16.05	Depart Burton Latimer for Pytchley
16.10	Arrive Pytchley House
	To be met by: Sir Gerald and Lady Glover
	Candidates and supporters from
	Corby, Daventry, Kettering, Northampton North
	and South and Wellingborough
16.30	Take-off from Pytchley by helicopter for Battersea
17.15	Arrive Battersea Heliport – transfer to cars
17.30	Arrive at Number Ten

Programme for Friday, 3 June 1983
VISIT TO WEST MIDLANDS AREA

08.15	Arrive Central Office
08.30 – 09.25	Prime Minister's Briefing Meeting
09.30 – 10.00	Daily News Conference – Ground Floor Conference Room
10.00 – 10.20	Private discussion between Prime Minister and Chairman
10.20	Provision for Media Interviews
10.50	Depart Central Office by car for Battersea Heliport
11.05	Helicopter to Stoneleigh Abbey, Kenilworth
11.50	Arrive Stoneleigh Abbey
	To be met by: Mrs Alma Hill, CBE – Area Chairman
	Mr L. Wolstenholme, BEM –
	.Central Office Agent

157

12.00	Meet and address Candidates and Party workers from the Coventry and Warwickshire Constituencies gathered at Stoneleigh Abbey
12.25	Leave Stoneleigh Abbey for Allesley Hotel in Campaign Coach
12.40	Arrive Allesley Hotel, Coventry Provision for Regional TV Interview Buffet lunch with Regional Editors – off the record
14.00	Depart Allesley Hotel for Aston Science Park
14.30	Arrive Aston Science Park To be met by: The Managing Director and representatives of the Birmingham City Council and the University
15.15	Depart Science Park for the NEC
15.35	Arrive *Birmingham Mail* Ideal Home Exhibition at the National Exhibition Centre for brief tour The Prime Minister will be invited to say a few words from a prepared rostrum
16.20	Depart Exhibition for the Metropole Hotel
16.25	Arrive Metropole Hotel – Manager Mr Graham Golby Time for speech preparation
18.00	Light supper in Suite
19.12	Leave Suite for the Rally in the Palace Suite of the Hotel accompanied by Mrs Hill and Mr Wolstenholme
19.15	West Midlands Area Rally Chairman: Mrs Alma Hill, CBE – Area Chairman
20.30	Approx. – Leave Metropole Hotel by car for London
22.00	Arrive Number Ten

Programme for Saturday, 4 June 1983
VISIT TO GREATER LONDON

10.25	Prime Minister to depart Number Ten by car (Campaign Coach leaves Central Office at 10.00 for Westminster North)
10.20	Campaign Coach arrives Westminster North Constituency
10.35	Prime Minister arrives Westminster North Constituency St John's Wood High Street, to meet the Candidate, John Wheeler, and make brief visit to local shopkeepers
10.55	Depart Westminster North
11.30	Arrive Ealing North Constituency To visit the Candidate, Harry Greenway, and campaign workers at Campaign Headquarters, Courthope Road, Greenford
11.45	Depart Ealing North
12.35	Arrive Hendon North Constituency To visit the Candidate, John Gorst, and campaign workers in the Shopping Area at The Broadway, Mill Hill, NW7
12.45	Depart Hendon North in cars (Campaign Coach and Press Coach return Central London)
13.00	Arrive Finchley Constituency Lunch at Campaign Headquarters, 212 Ballards Lane, Finchley, N3
13.30	Depart Campaign Headquarters for campaigning in Finchley
13.35	Finchley Central Shopping Area walkabout (Tesco area)
14.05	Depart
14.10	Street visit to Nether Court Avenue, N3
14.40	Depart

14.50	North Finchley Shopping Area walkabout (Owen Owen area)
15.05	Depart
15.10	Friern Barnet Shopping Area walkabout
15.20	Depart
15.25	Street visit to Friars Avenue and Manor Drive, N20
15.45	Depart
15.50	Street visit to Temple Avenue, N20, and gathering of Party workers at bottom of Temple Avenue
16.10	Depart Finchley
16.40	Arrive Hampstead and Highgate Constituency To visit the Candidate, Geoffrey Finsberg, and campaign workers at Campaign Headquarters, 36 College Crescent, NW3
16.50	Depart Hampstead
17.05	Arrive Number Ten

Programme for Sunday, 5 June 1983
YOUTH RALLY – WEMBLEY CONFERENCE CENTRE

10.00	Briefing for Television Interview
12.00	Arrive Number Twelve Downing Street – record 'Weekend World'
13.00	Return to Number Ten
14.40	Depart Number Ten for Wembley
15.00	Arrive Wembley Conference Centre To be met by: Mr Tim Cowell – Assistant Director, Youth Proceed to Chaucer Room via Canterbury Room To join: The Rt Hon. Cecil Parkinson – Chairman of the Party Mr Michael Spicer – Vice-Chairman
15.25	The Prime Minister and her party leave for the stage
15.35	Prime Minister to be announced by Party Chairman, and escorted to the rostrum by Mr Michael Spicer and Mr Tim Cowell Address Youth Rally at Wembley At the conclusion of her speech the Prime Minister will leave the rostrum and walk to acknowledge the Entertainers and Sportsmen The Prime Minister and her party to leave the stage and proceed to the Champion Bar for tea with the Entertainers and Sportsmen
16.25	Leave Champion Bar for Main Exit
16.30	Depart Wembley by car
17.00	Arrive Maddox St, W1 Record Party Electoral Broadcast Return to Number Ten
20.00	Supper in flat
20.30	Speech-writing

Programme for Monday, 6 June 1983
VISIT TO GREATER LONDON

08.00	Meeting with Robin Butler
08.15	Depart Number Ten for Central Office
08.30 – 09.25	Prime Minister's Briefing Meeting
09.30 – 10.00	Daily News Conference – Ground Floor Conference Room

159

10.00 – 10.20	Private discussion between Prime Minister and Chairman
10.20	ITN Interview
10.30	Depart Central Office by coach for John F. Renshaw & Co Limited
11.10	Arrive factory of John F. Renshaw & Co Limited (Mitcham and Morden Constituency) To be met by: Mrs Angela Rumbold – Candidate, Mitcham and Morden Mr John Rumbold Tour factory
11.40	Depart John F. Renshaw & Co Limited for Croydon North-West Constituency
11.50	Arrive Croydon North-West Constituency To meet the Candidate, Humphrey Malins, and helpers at Campaign Headquarters, 161 Brigstock Road, Thornton Heath
12.00	Depart Croydon North-West by car
12.30	Arrive Number Ten Lunch in flat Briefing for 'Granada 500'
15.00	Make-up
15.30	Depart Number Ten for Royalty Theatre, Aldwych
15.40	Approx. – arrive Royalty Theatre, Aldwych
16.00	Record 'Granada 500' Programme
16.30	Depart Royalty Theatre, Aldwych, for Number Ten – via House of Commons
17.00	Arrive Number Ten Speech-writing

Programme for Tuesday, 7 June 1983
NORTH WEST RALLY

08.25	Depart Number Ten for BBC Studios
08.45	Arrive BBC Studios (Lime Grove) Make-up if necessary
09.05	Record 'Election Call'
10.00	Depart BBC Studios for Number Ten Call in at Central Office if necessary Arrive Number Ten
13.00	Lunch in flat
14.10	Depart Number Ten for Maddox Street
14.30	Arrive Maddox Street – Record PEB
15.30	Depart Maddox Street for Victoria
16.00	Train from Victoria to Gatwick
17.00	Flight take-off from Gatwick Destination: Warton Aerodrome, Preston Flight Time: 1 hour
18.00	Arrive Warton Aerodrome, Preston Transfer to cars and depart for North Euston Hotel, Fleetwood
18.30	Arrive North Euston Hotel, Fleetwood To be met by: Mr Jim Cowpe and Mrs Moira Cowpe – Owners Mr Roger Johns and Mrs Hilary Johns – Owners Light meal in suite
19.10	Depart North Euston Hotel for Marine Hall, Fleetwood

19.17	Address Fylde Coast Rally
	Chairman: Mr Eric G. Taylor – Area Chairman
	The audience will have been present for about 25 minutes and an
	Appeal for funds will have been made and the collection taken
	At the end of the speech, the Chairman will propose a short vote
	of thanks
	The Party will proceed off the platform at the right-hand side
	(facing audience) in front of the stage, down the middle aisle and
	out through the entrance in the Wyre Lounge into waiting cars
20.15	Depart Marine Hall, Fleetwood, for Warton Aerodrome, Preston
21.00	Take-off from Warton Aerodrome
	Destination: Gatwick
	Flight Time: 1 hour
22.00	Arrive Gatwick – transfer to cars
23.00	Arrive Number Ten

Programme for Wednesday, 8 June 1983
VISIT TO WESSEX AREA

08.15	Arrive Central Office
08.30 – **09.25**	Prime Minister's Briefing Meeting
09.30 – **10.00 –**	Daily News Conference – Ground Floor Conference Room
10.00 – **10.20**	Private discussion between Prime Minister and Chairman
10.20	Provision for Media Interviews
10.55	Depart Central Office by car for Battersea Heliport
11.10	Flight take-off from Battersea Heliport Destination: Old Sarum Airfield Flying Time: 35 minutes
11.45	Arrive Old Sarum Airfield To be met by: Mr Robert Key – Candidate Salisbury Mrs Sue Key Mr Hugh Simmonds – Wessex Area Treasurer Mr David Roberts – Wessex Area COA Join Campaign Coach
11.50	Tour Edgley Aircraft Limited To be met by: Mr John Edgley – Chairman and Joint Managing Director Mr Bill Fraser – Joint Managing Director Mr Bill Purbrick – Sales Director
12.15	Demonstration flight by 'Optica' aircraft
12.25	Depart Edgley Aircraft Limited for Salisbury by Campaign Coach
12.45	Arrive The Guildhall Square, Market Place, Salisbury Unscheduled stop/walkabout/speak briefly to supporters
13.00	Depart The Guildhall Square for UK Provident House
13.10	Arrive UK Provident House, Castle Street, Salisbury
	To be met by: Mr S. G. Brooksbank, FCA – Chairman and Managing Director Mr A. Spedding, BSc, FIA, FSS, FIS – General Manager Buffet lunch
13.55	Tour Life Department and Visual Display Unit
14.10	Cross road to Computer Centre, Warner House

14.30	Depart UK Provident for Old Sarum Airfield
14.45	Take-off from Old Sarum Airfield for Isle of Wight by helicopter
15.00	Arrive British Hovercraft Corporation Limited

To be met by: Mrs Virginia Bottomley – Candidate Isle of Wight
Mr Edward Giles – Chairman Isle of Wight Cons. Assoc.
The Rt Hon. The Lord Aldington, KCMG, CBE, DSO, – Chairman British Hovercraft Corporation
Mr Richard Stanton-Jones – Deputy Chairman B.H.C.
Mr Basil Blackwell – Chief Executive B.H.C.

Tour works

1545	Depart British Hovercraft Corporation Limited
15.50 – 16.05	Unscheduled stop at seafront site adjacent to works to meet supporters
16.15	Take-off for Battersea Heliport
16.45	Arrive Battersea Heliport
17.00	Arrive Downing Street
18.30	Depart Downing Street for Finchley Constituency
19.15	Arrive Finchley Constituency for meeting at 57 Oakleigh Park North, N20, the home of Mr K. Patel
19.45	Depart
20.00	Arrive for meeting at 5 Hendon Avenue, N3, the home of Mrs Franks
20.30	Depart for Downing Street
21.15	Arrive Downing Street

Programme for Thursday, 9 June and Friday, 10 June (early a.m.) 1983
VISIT TO FINCHLEY

07.10	Depart Number Ten by car
07.15	Vote at Chelsea-Westminster Institute, Castle Lane, SW1
07.20	Return to Number Ten
08.30	Depart Number Ten by car for Finchley
09.15 – 13.00	Tour Committee Rooms
13.00	Return to Ballards Lane for lunch with key workers
15.00	(Approx.) Return to Number Ten
17.50	Interview at Number Ten with Bonnie Angelo, *Time* Magazine
18.00	Private appointment
23.00	(Approx.) Leave Number Ten for Finchley
23.40	Arrive Finchley At Hendon Town Hall, The Burroughs, Hendon, NW4

....

01.30	(Approx.) Declaration of result
02.00	(Approx.) Return to Ballards Lane
02.30	(Approx.) Return to Smith Square
03.00	(Approx.) Arrive Smith Square